Living from the Heart

By
Elizabeth MacDonald

Published by

ähäm

AHAM Publications
Asheboro, NC 27205
U.S.A.

Copyright © 2005

ISBN: 1-888599-31-6

(Printed in India)

Cover Art Design by Julie Peters

For further information, contact the publisher:

AHAM Publications • 4368 NC Hwy. 134
Asheboro, North Carolina 27205 • USA
Phone: (336) 381-3988 • Fax: (336) 381-3881
E-mail: ahamcntr@asheboro.com
Web site: www.aham.com

AHAM Publications is a division of the ASSOCIATION OF HAPPINESS FOR ALL MANKIND (AHAM) INC., a nonprofit spiritual education organization.

Living from the Heart

... It's All About Love

A Self-Inquiry Experience

September 17, 2005

Tina,
Follow your Heart
all the way the Home.

♡ Elizabeth
MacDonald

Dedication

This book is respectfully dedicated to all who have been open and eager to receive a fresh, new perspective ... thus Living Free ... as love, as peace, as a deep inner joy and delight ... from their own Power of Awareness

Appreciation

I wish to express my appreciation and heartfelt gratitude to all who worked together to compile and arrange these talks to create a simple presentation for all to experience.

I especially wish to thank James Rogers, Linda Swanson, Richard Fletcher, Andrea Katzer, Ron Whitaker, Atma-Kirsten Skytte Christiansen, Scott Fallows and Jim Dillinger.

Contents

Foreword

"Whatever effort that puts the mind inward is a positive move towards being the Truth – the ego-I merging with the Self-I, the I AM," said Bhagavan Ramana.

In that light, one feels happy that the useful "sharings" that Elizabeth MacDonald has had with earnest seekers during these years, have been collected and presented in a book-form: *Living From The Heart*. It is always a praiseworthy endeavor to help the turbulent minds turn within and peacefully rest in the Truth of one's own Heart. While clearing the valid doubts of the striving seekers, it is a healthy move that Elizabeth has taken, carefully too, not to project herself as the "manufacturer" of the Truth (which, unfortunately, the New Age masters are indulging in). She honestly shares the Truth, as Truth, by truthfully turning the questioner's mind inwards ("180 degrees turn," as she aptly calls it) to one's own Heart, as the One and only Truth. This is a very laudable achievement, indeed!

The dialogues are lively, down-to-earth and yet transcending the limitations of logical, intellectual, psychological and psychical impositions and tall claims usually brought about and dealt with at various levels of the limping minds. The author through her good grasp of the Direct Teaching of Bhagavan Ramana – "Self-Inquiry" – repeatedly and successfully drives home the imminent need for waking up to the Truth – "I AM" – in one's own Heart, for all forms of questions raised by many a "doubting Thomases!" *Kaivalya Navaneeta*, an authentic Advaitic Tamil text, emphasizes the absolute necessity for the earnest seekers to continuously ponder over the Truth and relentlessly share it among fellow-seekers.

Living From The Heart is a handy, beautiful, reference book for the "inward journey" of all true seekers.

"Love (*Bhakti*) is the mother of Wisdom (*Jnana*) – *Jnana Mata*," repeatedly asserted Bhagavan Ramana. The seeker has this "union" (*Yoga*) in one's Heart, as direct experience. And, this book helps one move towards this irreversible union.

V. Ganesan
Former Editor of *The Mountain Path*
Ananda Ramana
Tiruvannamalai, South India
February 1, 2005

Introduction

The title of this book, *Living from the Heart*, was inspired by the following quote of Bhagavan Ramana from *Talks with Sri Ramana Maharshi*.

> *Only if one knows the truth of love, which is the real nature of Self, will the strong entangled knot of life be untied. Only if one attains the height of love will liberation be attained. Such is the heart of all religions. The experience of Self is only love, which is seeing only love, hearing only love, feeling only love, tasting only love and smelling only love, which is bliss.*

> *Love is not different from the Self. Love of an object is of an inferior order and cannot endure. Whereas the Self is Love, in other words, God is Love.*

This book is comprised primarily of actual transcriptions of live "Heart Line" programs – a meditation program held over the telephone in the late '90s on a group bridge line call (called "Heart Line") guided by Elizabeth, and then followed up by questions from the participants.

The Heart Line calls were mainly for new people interested in Self-Inquiry and wanting "a taste" of it. The calls gave participants an opportunity to experience the inner Stillness that Self-Inquiry leads one into, without themselves having to know experientially or understand fully all the facets of the process. There were also times when the calls were with the graduates of the AHAM programs, those who were already practicing the Self-Inquiry in their day-to-day lives.

AHAM, the Association of Happiness for All Mankind, is dedicated to disseminating Self-Inquiry. "Self-Inquiry is the simplest and most direct method to experience and abide in the Self," or Core of Existence, first shared with the world by Bhagavan Sri Ramana Maharshi (hereinafter "Bhagavan Ramana"), commencing about 100 years ago in India. This Core, which Sri Bhagavan Ramana called the Heart, is the "Kingdom of God within us," that Jesus speaks of, and which is referred to in the scriptures of many religions. The Heart is also referred to as Source, Awareness, I AM, or Being. Elizabeth, who is AHAM's Senior Trainer, along with her teacher, A. Ramana (hereinafter "Ramana"), AHAM's Spiritual Director, has guided countless spiritual seekers to experience this radiance of pure Awareness as their own Being, through Self-Inquiry.

The material in this book presents a dynamic "in-the-moment" experience of Self-Inquiry. As you read, you may feel a familiar stirring within you, touching your Inner Being allowing you to re-cognize, or "know again," that which has been hidden until now. Keep in mind that words can only act as signposts, pointing you in the right direction, therefore avoid getting caught up in definitions, references, or comparisons to what you may already "know."

During the guided meditations, you will see a series of three dots (...) suggesting a momentary pause, inviting you to participate in the meditation by giving you the experience of relaxing into the Heart.

The symbol ♥♥♥♥♥♥ suggests a longer pause, to give yourself time to be with the material you've just read, to fully experience the Heart, your Natural State of Being.

As a further enhancement of your experience before reading, it is also suggested that you listen to a Guided Meditation by Elizabeth, from the *Replenish Series* of tapes listed at the end of this book .

As you read this book, delight in your awakening in this Love and fully enjoy ... *Living from the Heart.*

Namasté

I honor That Place in you
where the whole universe resides,
That Place of Love, Peace, Joy and Light.
And as you Abide in That Place in you
and I Abide in That Place in me,
there is not-two,
there is only One of Us.

Elements of
Self-Inquiry

The ultimate or highest purpose of every [meditation] method is to finally give you the strength to still or quiet the mind, thus turning it inward to merge in the Self, which itself is real God, the Source of Consciousness ... Self-Inquiry takes you immediately or directly to the truth, from the very beginning.

A. Ramana,
There is Neither I, Nor Other Than I, There is Only ... [p. 185]
AHAM Publications, Asheboro,
North Carolina, USA, 1999

A Heart Line Experience

"Heart Line" is what we call this connection. You're calling in to the AHAM Meditation Retreat Center. I'm Patricia. Many of you I've spoken with before. In a moment I'll be introducing you to Elizabeth MacDonald, AHAM's senior trainer. She'll be conducting the program this evening. Before we begin, I'd like to share with you the purpose of AHAM and our teaching.

AHAM's purpose is "to transform your awareness of who you really are, so as to create a space in consciousness that is clear, that enables you to experience living, so that what is usually upsetting you, that is, what you've been trying to change or have been putting up with, is worked out and cleared up just in the process of living life itself. Then, steady, unshakable Happiness remains as your natural state."

So consider these questions for yourself. Do you have something you've been trying to change, or have been putting up with in your life? And are you interested in transforming those areas that you've been tolerating so that they're no longer affecting you?

♥♥♥♥♥♥♥

Are you interested in *total* transformation? To awakening to *who you really are,* to your True Self? Are you choosing for this awakened awareness to be integrated into your daily life with consistency?

♥♥♥♥♥♥

This is what our AHAM programs are all about.

AHAM was founded in 1978, by A. Ramana and Elizabeth MacDonald. They've been working together more than 25 years, sharing this process of Self-Inquiry. It's a Conscious transformational process for realization and abidance in the True Self, who you really are. This simple, Conscious process was introduced to the world by Bhagavan Sri Ramana Maharshi. Many have come to a spiritual awakening through this Self-Inquiry process.

And now I would like to introduce you to Elizabeth. She'll conduct a Self-Inquiry meditation that will give you a chance to participate in and experience the process. Relax into this process and receive that which you truly are.

Elizabeth: Welcome to Heart Line. And welcome to the Heart experience that we here at AHAM call, "Conscious Company," or "Sat Sanga" as it's known in Sanskrit. I would like to start with a guided meditation.

♥♥♥♥♥♥

Be aware now of whatever is occurring in your space, including all that is now in your awareness ... and allow it to be there, just as it is. Even though we're all in different parts of the country, we're all together here on this line of communication. There may be a lot going on around each one of us in our personal space, so whatever we're aware of now, allow it to be there, just as it is. ... This practice or process isn't about closing out the world – it's about *including* it all in your awareness, and allowing it to be entirely OK, whatever it is.

♥♥♥♥♥♥

Now, be aware of your breath ... allowing it to flow through the body as it normally does ... Just be aware of the breath by watching it ... for breath and thought arise from the same source. When you quietly watch the breath, it will begin to slow down ... and the thoughts may even begin to slow down or subside as well. In this process, we are able to locate the source of breath, and the source of thought, and feel the sense of "I-I" as Awareness *itself*.

Whatever thoughts are occurring right now, allow them to just drift by. Do not follow them, but choose to find the source of thought ... Choose to locate within you *that which is*, before anything else can be ... We do this with the Self-Inquiry process ... Who is thinking? Who is breathing? Who is listening? I am. I ... I ... I ...

Do we know what this "I" is? Most of the time we take it for granted. But now, in this process, we investigate into this "I" ... I exist, and I am conscious of my existence ... "Who am I?"

Now just feel the "I" ... Feel this existence ... this consciousness ... this "I." And in feeling only this "I," our attention is automatically drawn, focused inward, into the spiritual Heart ... the Core of our Being.

So just feel "I" as existence-consciousness ... as just the "I-I" Awareness. It will automatically draw your attention inward, into the Source, into the Heart, into That which is before anything else can be.

Abide as That ... here and now ... in this moment, in the silence, in the stillness of the Heart. Dive in now, into this stillness and silence ...

♥♥♥ ♥♥♥♥

Realize the Truth in this moment: that while we are each in this Heart-to-Heart connection, certainly our bodies are in different places around the world ... But here we are connected, in the true essence of Being, in the Truth of who we *really* are ... *prior* to the body ... *prior* to the mind.

Allow this experience to awaken deeply as we remain in the Silence of the Heart together ...

♥♥♥♥♥♥

Now take a couple of deep breaths. Allow this quality to fully permeate your whole body as you breathe in deeply and fully receive the radiance of the Heart. Feel it fully and completely, throughout the whole body-mind ... as you breathe it through you ... like liquid energy.

If it feels comfortable to do so, then open your eyes ... or you can keep them closed throughout the call, whichever suits you, as this call is either an eyes-open or eyes-closed meditation. It is mainly for us to keep our attention *only* in the Heart; this is the true spiritual work. No matter what we're doing, no matter what's occurring around us, see how we are also able to keep our connection with the inner Source of our Being. So as we continue the call, if there's anyone who would like to share their experience or ask a question, I'd be happy to be with you in that now.

Participant: You mentioned that thought and breath arise from the same source. Could you talk a bit more about that?

Elizabeth: Sri Bhagavan Ramana Maharshi writes about it. But the best thing is for you to experience it for yourself. As you are breathing right now, ask or observe, "Who's thinking, and who's breathing?"

Participant: I can't. I can't see the thinker. My thoughts just seem to appear.

Elizabeth: Who's thinking those thoughts?

Participant: I don't see it.

Elizabeth: Do you *feel* it? Do you feel the "I" that is thinking those thoughts, and the "I" that is breathing? Do you feel that "I?"

Participant: Not really. They both just seem to happen on their own.

Elizabeth: OK, so they're happening on their own. To whom are they happening, or seem to be happening to, or with? Who is seeing and saying this? Is there not an "I" there that is thinking and breathing? An "I" that is seeing and saying this?

Participant: I guess there must be.

Elizabeth: You're not sure? Do you deny that you are there? That you exist? Who says so? Who says that *"you"* guess there must be?

Participant: I do.

Elizabeth: Yes! That very "I" is the one; it is being used every day. You call it "I." You say, "I'm breathing, I'm thinking, I'm doing, I'm walking, I'm talking." But do we know what this "I" is? Investigate into this "I," which is an immediate thing *now*, not reading about it, or thinking *about* it ... but right now, investigate into this "I." If you were in a pitch black room right now – pitch black – and you couldn't see your hand in front of your face, you couldn't even see your body, and I was standing outside the room and asked you, "Is my book in there?" What would you say? Do you know? Would it be there?

Participant: I wouldn't know.

Elizabeth: Right! But, if I were to say, "Are *you* in there?"

Participant: Ok, now I get it; there's the sense of "I."

Elizabeth: Yes. Now, get a hold of that sense of "I." Hold onto that sense of "I," because that's the key. And withdraw or trace your attention, or the "I" back into its source, out of which the "I" appears or arises. And then, of course, second to that are the other thoughts, breathing, and everything else. That's the very key here. Got it?

Participant: Yes, I believe I do.

Elizabeth: Good. Now, just stay with this process as we continue in the call, because, we're already in the Inquiry process. Stay with this "I – feeling" alone, and it will draw your attention back into the source, or use it as an indicator as you intentionally trace it back to its source.

♥♥♥♥♥♥

Next Participant: You spoke about abiding in the Heart. Is this a location?

Elizabeth: No. There is, of course, the physical heart that pumps blood in the body, but what we're talking about here is in regard to the spiritual Heart, which doesn't really have a location in the physical body. It is a felt sense of presence, or radiance that can be felt on the right side of the chest, although it's not really in the physical body itself. The infinite eternal Being, the Heart, is not encapsulated in the body, whatsoever.

It is like "being a sponge in the ocean, and the ocean is in the sponge." The sponge would be like our body-mind, and the ocean is like the Self or the Heart. The Self is what gives life to that sponge; it's permeating through it and giving life to it, so to speak. It's not located in the body, though it seems to be.

As you experience the "I" and you continue to feel that "I-sense," you may get a sensation in the right side of your chest, a radiant quality, a lightness, or a fullness, that's like a love feeling, a feeling of acceptance, an "OK-ness" feeling throughout. That is what the Heart feels like. Just stay with that. That "I" is the focus, that "felt I" presence or "I AM" radiance becomes the focus.

Instead of attention being on worries, concerns, or thoughts, attention is brought to this quality, or this radiance, and we just remain with this underlying quality that's here and present all the time. And, without that, nothing can be, so we keep our attention *Here.* Everything happens from that point or "place." In my experience, it's the best way to live day-to-day in my life.

In the Christian faith, it's taught to "let go and let God." That's what we're doing by surrendering everything to the Heart and letting *It* be what directs our life.

Participant: You said to let everything go, to *allow everything.* But part of me says, "No, No!"

Elizabeth: Yes, I understand. Now, look to see just what's saying "No." What is it? It's the mind. It is *that* which is going on in the mind, in the outward-turned direction of your consciousness. Your attention right now is literally riveted toward and identified with the world and its objects.

But when you feel the "I-I," or the feeling of the pure "I AM," your attention is magnetically drawn toward the Heart. So, it is attention going outward that is being challenged. The whole configuration or pattern is being challenged. The ego, the body-mind, all the conditioned patterns, the sense of separation from the true Self, the "I" wanting to "do it my way" – all of that is being challenged.

So the mind and ego will put up a powerful fight, not wanting you to go in this inner direction. But once you've had a clear sense of it, it's like a bloodhound dog on a scent. Once it's got the scent of its master, or some subject, it just stays with it until it finds him. In the same way, we must come to that place, and to that time in our life, where we make the choice to truly choose the Self, or real Happiness, and stay with the inwardness of the mind, which will eventually "locate" it.

As it says in the Bible, "Choose you this day whom you will serve. As for me and my house, we will serve the Lord." We must make the choice to serve the Lord, or God within, first, to locate within us the Source, the Self, *That which is*, and must be, before anything else can be. Then our life is conducted from That Source, rather than from the separate ego or body-mind and its conditioned patterns, and all that is limiting oneself, which is now superimposing itself on the Self. In AHAM, we call this "choosing Happiness-NOW. "

Happiness is our True Nature. Freedom is our True Nature. Choose it. Choose it *now*. When you choose it now, you can use the Inquiry to make a shift to the inward flow of consciousness, and thereby allow this to be what is now present and real in your life, once and for all.

We have to start with this choice. When anything else comes up, say to your self, "No thank you! I'm not going

there. I'm choosing happiness. I'm choosing freedom."
And make that connection with the Self. Go Home –
"Home is where the Heart is."

♥♥♥♥♥♥♥

Next Participant: You mentioned earlier that our
happiness is independent of outer events and
circumstances. Would you explain that?

Elizabeth: Happiness is our True Nature. Just as
the nature of water is wet, and fire is hot, happiness is
our true nature.   Abiding in the awakened Self – not as
a mere belief or philosophy – we won't continue to look
for happiness outside the Self in the world – in people,
places and things. Rather, we will bring our happiness
to the world, to the people in our lives. And then there
won't be the continued disappointments, the expectations,
the demands on life to "give" us what we want. Wants
and expectations are forms of suffering, because
sometimes you get what you want and sometimes
you don't.

Now you can continue being in this true nature
of Happiness, which is the Self that you are, and feel
the fullness of this constantly, moment-to-moment
without interruption, steady and unshakable. Nothing
can disturb it.

♥♥♥♥♥♥

Participant: I was just wondering about this, because
I read something in the paper this morning that was
horrible, really graphic. So, it's really hard for me to
imagine that this happiness is unshakable. There is so
much that is horrible happening in the world. Yet, you're
saying it is possible.

Elizabeth: Yes, it is possible. There is a pure, prior Awareness that's occurring *right now*. And this still, silent Being that we are, always is and has to be present *before* anything else can be.   The analogy we often use in our programs to describe this comes from Ramana Maharshi, the one who originated Self-Inquiry. He gives the example of a film projector. There's the film in the projector, which projects the movie events onto the screen. But what must be there *first* before the film will shine onto the screen?

Participant: The light.

Elizabeth: Yes, the light. So the film is the body-mind configuration and the world represents the pictures projected on the screen. It will change. It will come and go with many scenes. But the light *prior to it* is pure, it is unaffected by the film – it has never been touched by the film. The Awareness, like the light, is what illumines the world through the film of the mind, projecting it out onto the screen of life. Be this light of Awareness, of the Heart, and be happy!

♥♥♥ ♥ ♥♥

Another example is that all the perceived horror of this world does not affect you when you are asleep; it is only present in the waking and dream states. It is in the mind only, and not present when the mind is not active. You, the Self, are present in deep sleep, but the world is not. Stay in that quality of pure Being that you are while sleeping, while remaining awake, and be happy.

Namasté.

Remain Here in Awareness

Following a guided meditation by Elizabeth ...

Participant: When, in the meditation, you say "Being in the Heart," do you mean for us to focus inside our heart – our actual physical organ of the heart?

Elizabeth: No. The Heart is a term that is used by Ramana Maharshi quite frequently. It's the spiritual Heart; it's not the heart that pumps blood. This practice isn't about finding that location anywhere in the body. It's about being what we *are* and then allowing that to reveal itself to us. It's not actually experienced in the body-mind itself, but it can sometimes feel like a warmth or a glow in the center of the chest. However, we're not focusing on this particular spot during our meditation.

Right now in this moment, as you're being here in this conversation, isn't there an Awareness that's aware of your body-mind sitting there, listening to this conversation and whatever experience that's occurring? Isn't there an Awareness that's Here, seeing all that's there?

♥♥♥♥♥♥

Participant: Yes.

Elizabeth: Okay. Now if you'll just be with that Awareness that's Here, just for a moment, and tune in to what that feels like. Are you with me?

Participant: Yes. It's hard to separate the Awareness from my judging mind.

Elizabeth: But isn't that Awareness *aware* of the judging mind?

Participant: Yes.

Elizabeth: So, *it's Here,* seeing the judging mind *there,* right?

Participant: Right.

Elizabeth: Okay. So stay *Here,* right Here. And anything that comes and goes *there,* see that it's not you. It certainly can't be you if you're Here seeing it there. So as long as you can see it *there,* it's not you. It's in your Awareness, but it's not you. If we investigate into this Awareness, really dive into it, as Ramana Maharshi says, "Like a salt doll diving into the ocean," we get this perspective once and for all, as our own direct realization. In this practice that is all we do. That's what we meditate constantly. We keep our attention constantly on this Awareness, which we call the Heart, the Self, or whatever you choose to call it, it doesn't really matter. It's the *experience,* the direct realization of it. So the Inquiry is the tool for us to take our attention off of the body-mind and bring it back to what we really are as this Prior Awareness

♥♥♥♥♥♥

Participant: As you say we are already that Awareness, and yet to stay aware of it seems to take a tremendous amount of effort, because we're not normally putting our attention there. Our attention usually goes outward instead of inward on what you are implying that we already are. It seems to take a tremendous amount of effort that I'm not sure I'm capable of. And that if I do get it, it will be totally by accident!

Elizabeth: I understand. We give an entire Self-Inquiry Series that gives you instruction on how to stay in this Awareness.

Participant: I've only just begun reading a few of Ramana Maharshi's books, and this program is dovetailing with my readings very nicely. I like the whole process.

Elizabeth: Oh, so you're reading Ramana Maharshi? Wonderful! That's the place to start.

Participant: I have a question. I'd like to know how much time you would recommend per day for a person just starting this method of meditation. I've meditated for many years, but I haven't used this technique.

Elizabeth: In the morning and evening, in the beginning; just as you wake up in the morning and just before you go to bed at night is good. But that's only in the beginning. Eventually, with instruction, you learn to Inquire *constantly*. How long of a period have you sat in meditation up to this point?

Participant: Well, I've meditated for up to an hour many times, but it's generally about 30 to 45 minutes.

Elizabeth: That's a good amount of time. If you can do that, that's great. The longer the better, in the sense that often when we sit to meditate our minds are very active and then we get up and begin our day, and don't have time to settle into the stillness where real transformation occurs. So having 45 minutes to an hour is very conducive to having this time to "settle in."

Just before you go to bed is a great time to meditate, because you're releasing whatever occurred during the day and entering sleep with an empty mind. Then you wake up fresh and ready for your morning meditation. If you continue this cycle it's very beneficial.

For those wanting Self-realization, or Liberation from all identification with the body-mind as being the Self, and freedom from the addiction to thought, then Self-Inquiry is practiced, until there is no sense of a separate "I" remaining. The results are that one is merged in the pure Self, or the transcendental Awareness that *is* the Self.

♥♥♥♥♥♥♥

Participant: I have another question. I notice for myself that, especially at the beginning of meditation, many thoughts come up. With your technique of meditation, are you just barely noticing the thoughts?

Elizabeth: As you notice the thoughts coming up, do the Inquiry: "Who's thinking? Who's the thinker of these thoughts?" The only possible answer is "I am; it is me." It always comes back to the "I." Or, if you're meditating and there's an emotion there, ask "Who's having this sadness or upset or whatever the upset is?" "*I am.*"

When you ask the question "Who am I?", just rest with that. Don't fill in the space with, "I'm a child of God," or "I am the Heart," or "I am Bill Smith," etc. With the question, you *are* Inquiring and redirecting the mind or consciousness into, or investigating into that "I." "I" am thinking right now, or "I" am angry, or "I" am sad, etc. Ask, "Who am I?" and follow the "I-feeling" back to its inner Source, the location out of which the "I-thought," or "I-emotion," or "I-feeling" came up originally. Then abide in this prior Stillness and Silence. That is the practice.

♥♥♥♥♥♥♥

Participant: I would love to seek and find enlightenment in this life. And by that I mean Self-realization, to find out who I really am. I'm wondering if an intense desire to do that helps in this process.

Elizabeth: Yes, it does initially. And then there comes a time to end the search. We can get into a vicious cycle and get caught up and stuck in the searching.

Participant: You mean ending the search outwardly?

Elizabeth: Yes, outwardly – such as in trying to find something else that is believed to work better, another teaching, another teacher, another group, and continue searching for something to "work" for you. Seeking then becomes a strategy of the mind to stay intact and in control.

It's time to end the search, make that connection and go home, to "be here now," constantly in the Awareness. It is "The Enlightened Way of Happiness Now," being Here now, in the Heart, sitting *Here* and no longer straying away.

♥♥♥♥♥♥♥

Participant: Why is it that some people seem to do this better than others? It seems like some people are riper when they start than others.

Elizabeth: That's a good question. Look at Bhagavan Sri Ramana Maharshi. He was 16 years old. He had a death experience and immediately inquired, and asked himself "Who am I?" And that was *it*. It was over in that moment. The episode of his entire spiritual practice or process took only about 20 minutes. So, obviously he came into this lifetime with very little to work out; he was already very ripe.

Ramana had an experience of the Self, following an accident as a child, but lost it. His quest continued. He was finally enlightened after years of spiritual practice, on seeing a picture of Sri Ramana Maharshi, and using the Inquiry to stabilize the final event. This was back in 1973. He is one who when he gets a hold of something and he knows it works, he works it with full determination. That's all it takes.

So everything we do here in our Center, in our Conscious Curriculum, is all about that. It's about "taking the bull by the horns." People like yourself are the ones who are drawn here; the ones who say: "I want to get it in this lifetime." That's *it!*

Participant: Yes. And what did Ramana Maharshi mean when he said that this shouldn't be used as a mantra?

Elizabeth: He meant that this is an active process. If you start using it as a mantra, repeating the question "Who am I?" over and over, then you're just in the mind; you're not in the transformational process. It's just going around and around in the mind. That would then be a strategy the mind would use to avoid following the Inquiry all the way through to dissolving the mind's conditioned patterns into the Heart. And so the mind would still be in charge.

Participant: For this to really work then, we need to use it in our waking life with every situation that comes up?

Elizabeth: Absolutely. It's a *constant* practice, moment-to-moment.

Participant: It's not used just two times a day when you sit down to meditate.

Elizabeth: Your morning and evening meditations are a time to get a good footing, a good start. It's a good way to begin and end the day, in the Heart, and then choose to stay "here" while life goes on. Then, if and when you get pulled back out into the mind, you can be on top of it and just do the Inquiry. So your sit-down meditations are beneficial, but they are not enough. They give you a good footing and are a good time to practice sitting in the Heart. But you must move towards "sitting" or abiding in the Heart moment-to-moment.

Next Participant: First of all, it seems like it takes great surrender to do this. Not so much effort as surrender. The effort seems to be just letting go of the fear of surrendering, if that makes sense.

Elizabeth: Yes.

Participant: And do you lose your compassion for others?

Elizabeth: Absolutely not.

Participant: It's almost like I have to be involved in their drama to be compassionate.

Elizabeth: No, that's not it at all. If your friend is going through a particular situation, you can be right "in their shoes" with them, but you're *Here* in the Heart *prior* to the body-mind and its reactions.

It's like you're watching it on TV, or watching a movie. You're very present, but you know it's just a movie. That's one way to describe it. Actually, for me, the compassion is even greater, because I'm not stuck in my own resistance or identification while the person needs me to be there with him. It is how I can *truly be* with someone. In the past, I would be more present with what was going on in *me*, rather than being able to be with my friend.

So, while "sitting in the Heart," nothing outside really changes. Life still looks the same, but the way you connect or relate with it is different. You just are not caught up in it anymore. It can be very close to you, in your Awareness, but there is a space there, and you know it is *not* you. So you can really be okay with what comes up in the moment, with yourself and with everyone else, being with it in acceptance, compassion, and sensitivity. All the good qualities that are *natural* can now be expressed. So it's a very ordinary thing when enlightenment "occurs." It's nothing extra-ordinary at all in the appearance of things, except for one small thing which is actually pretty major: you are no longer at the *effect* of life. You are completely okay with whatever comes up. It's unconditional love ... that's a good way to describe it. It's the Truth of who you are.

Now, just stay right *Here*.

Namasté.

What Feels True for You?

Following a guided meditation by Elizabeth ...

Participant: Meditation is a whole new process for me, so I'm trying not to analyze it so much as feel it. But at the same time, I feel that there's some need to think about it, to look into it a little bit.

I get a sense there are two different things that have to happen here. One part of me fears that I need to somehow work through the "language" of this process, as it seems to have its own unique language. The other part of me feels that it's the Heart, just simply the Heart, which is where I *tend* to want to be. I tend to want to, right now in my life, just open my Heart. And I don't want to intellectualize things. But I keep hearing this language "prior to." So where's the balance?

Elizabeth: Well, the words are not important. The most important thing is the experience of the Heart ... and the rest of it will just fall into place. When I first met Ramana years ago I didn't understand any of the words he used. And yet, there was a *qualitative* experience that I felt when we were together, and that's what I gave my attention to. Are you feeling that right now? Are you experiencing the Heart right now?

Participant: Yes.

Elizabeth: That's what we give our devotion to, our attention to – our *full* attention to. All the Inquiry is, is a tool, a mechanism to keep our attention Here. Our attention wants to go outward onto thought, as you're saying: analyzing, or trying to figure things out, or fix things, or make things better for yourself or the people around you. And very little attention is going toward the Heart, toward the Self, or whatever you want to call it. In this case, we're calling it the Heart.

So, Self-Inquiry is the tool that keeps us remembering the Heart, because that's our base – our field and ground of Being. Without that, nothing can be. So we want to keep it simple. And the words are not important.

Participant: I like that, and that's where I want to be. That is what I believe is all that's needed. Yet, when I went last night to the meeting I saw a book by Ramana and I thought to myself, "Why all that language to explain it?"

Elizabeth: Well, he's not really explaining it. When you're reading the words of someone who is coming from the Heart it's like a tuning fork resonating a particular note. Ramana is coming *from* it; he's not talking *about* it intellectually. As you read the books or listen to the tapes, just tune into the *quality*. Bhagavan Ramana says, "Silence is the perennial flow of language." It isn't what is being said, it's what the words are pointing to.

And if you're already able to stay in that Silence, then that's where your focus should be. Remain Here and then everything else will come to you as it did for me as time went on. The intellect began to realize what the Heart already knew. It's just a different approach. Different people have different approaches to this process. Either they come at it from the Heart directly, or they come at it from the intellect into the Heart. It's fine either way.

But the Inquiry is the key. It's a simple step-by-step process to keep you ever abiding in the Heart, because that's all there is.

Participant: I feel overwhelmed. I just had tears in my eyes and a feeling of "overwhelming-ness."

Elizabeth: Allow that – it's your Heart opening to receive the Truth ... the simple Truth.

♥♥♥♥♥♥

Next Participant: I gradually settled into the silence, and I was able to keep thoughts away. I mean, the thoughts came in, and they just passed by. What I feel right now is this space where we are – the special space – and I feel the need to be able to make that continual. My question, I guess, is how can I continually stay in this space rather than pass in and out of it throughout my day as I face all the tension and the demands, so they won't crowd in and engulf me again, as they always do.

Elizabeth: That's where Self-Inquiry as a practice comes in. Now that you know what the stillness is, you know that it is possible for you to be in the Heart. It is simply what you *are*. That's what we all are. It is always Here. What happens is that when we go into our life situations, our attention goes outward toward the thinking process the emotions, and we try to work it from this base which is separate from the Heart.

We leave the Heart behind, and we don't include it in our day-to-day attention. We leave it behind and separate from it and go in the outward direction. So the Self-Inquiry gives us an opportunity to include it, to let the Heart actually be the *base* from which we operate.

Now, it *does* take practice to do that, and the Inquiry is the tool. Its premise is that in order for me to be conscious of anything, first I must be *conscious*. That consciousness that "*I AM,*" what is that? Once I get the experience of what that is, I stay with the consciousness that *"I AM."* Without that consciousness, nothing else can be. Feel this *"*I AM*"* ...

♥♥♥♥♥♥

This Consciousness is always with you; it's always Here. It is *You*. It's aware of everything that's occurring right now, watching. It's aware. It's conscious of everything. So, include that Consciousness in your being aware of everything.

Remain *as* that Consciousness, *as* that Awareness, as the Heart *right now,* as you are going about what you need to do. And the Inquiry brings you back if you do find yourself getting caught up in people, places and things, or whatever is going on. You use it to come back to this conscious presence that you are experiencing right now. You can do it with your eyes open. Whether your eyes are open or your eyes are closed, you're conscious. You're even conscious in the dream you had last night. *You* saw that dream; *you* were aware of that dream. This Conscious Awareness is Here all the time. It never sleeps. It is always awake. That is the connection that you're making now.

♥♥♥♥♥♥

Next Participant: I just wanted to thank you for that wonderful meditation. It's been quite a challenge for me coming back to the States, with all the stimulation here. It's much easier for me to be in India. I have so much coming up right now around finding a job, finding a new home ... it's easy to bring attention *outward.* So I need this support to direct me back inward as much as possible.

Elizabeth: Yes, there is a lot of support for you in the Continued Practice home-study program.

Next Participant: I've been to India myself. I've done lots of this kind of thing. But I guess I don't understand what you mean by Self-Inquiry.

Elizabeth: Self-Inquiry is a practice. Actually it's a mechanism, like a switch. When you use the Self-Inquiry as an actual practice, in its step-by-step process, it switches your attention from the outward flow into the inward flow, into the Heart. It is a very simple process. It continues to keep your attention in Awareness, in the Self.

Participant: That is great! A true way to remind me to be in the Awareness, all the time.

Elizabeth: As Awareness there is no coming and going. There is only the Heart. There is only the Silence. That is what we are. That is the completion, ... the final key.

Namasté.

Say "Yes" to What Is!

This talk is starting with a guided meditation. Read slowly and follow the process into the Stillness and Peace of the Heart.

Elizabeth: What is present in your space? What is here now? What is real? What is true?

Yes, there's a body, there's breath and breathing, there's sound. All the senses are here as windows of perception of what we call the world, tuning us into what is in our space right now ... Accept it all just as it is.

In this meditation we are tuning in to what is *Real*, to what is True, to That which moves *prior* to this body-mind configuration, prior to the senses, prior to everything that is objective and so-called "real." We are coming into the Heart and reacquainting ourselves with That which *Is*.

We begin this by allowing whatever is here to just be here.

So often we deny, or avoid, or fight with that which is present, wishing it wasn't here, wishing there was something different. But here and now, in this Conscious Company, we're saying "Yes" to what is present, allowing it to be here just as it is. This is the true practice of living in the Heart. Feel this "Yes" to what is there now in your Awareness ...

♥♥♥♥♥♥

And once one is tuned in to this, it becomes more than just a practice. We realize it's what we *are*. That which we are says "Yes" to what is present in the moment. And this allows full acceptance, full unconditional love to be present. For there is no identification with what is there in our Awareness.

The Heart is already free of what we are perceiving, of what we are aware of. So as we are Here ... now ... being aware of what is present in our awareness, if our attention is being drawn to thoughts, to sensations, to experiences, just notice that.

Again, not avoiding any of it, not fighting with it, but saying "Yes" to it.

♥♥♥♥♥♥

Yes, thinking is going on. Don't try to change it, or try to do anything with it whatsoever that would further the identification with it. That's the magic of saying "Yes." It lets it *be*.

And, with Inquiry, we utilize whatever is taking our attention outward to bring our attention inward, to this place of acceptance and love.

Who is thinking? Who is experiencing? "I" am. Who is the thinker of these thoughts? Who's experiencing this experience? "I" am.

Do we know who this "I" really is? We say "I." We refer to that very often. But do we know who this "I" really is?

Now is the time to investigate into this "I" to really discover, reveal, and realize, or make real what this "I" actually is with this question, "Who am I? ... I-I-I." Feel and follow this I-I-I inward. Relax into this inward flow of Consciousness ...

Be fully consumed by Silence ... Stillness ... the Heart. Give way to it ... Fully receive it ...

It's always been here ... right Here ...

♥♥♥♥♥♥

At some point a thought may come up. Don't follow that thought. In this moment, right here, right now we're abiding in our True Nature ... We're realizing we are already That ... And all thought that would say we're *not* That is being dissolved, dispelled ... Just like when we turn on the light the darkness disappears. The "light switch" is this question that was given to us by Bhagavan Ramana: WHO AM I? Be with this question, unmoved. Feel I-I ...

♥♥♥♥♥♥

You may be experiencing a releasing, a melting away of the body-mind identification. Give full permission to the body-mind to have whatever experience that is occurring ... and is now being erased in the presence of the Truth, in the presence of the Heart, in this radiance, in this Fire of Consciousness that is Here and Now present.

All that is not That burns away. Say "Yes" to that, and it all burns away, just like the sun burning away the clouds on a cloudy day. *Be* the radiance of the sun, the Self, the Heart that we are ... no longer identifying with clouds, so to speak, or that which is objective.

That which is "out" there, is *there*. I am *Here*, as this Radiance of the Heart. Remain *Here* and just let whatever is going on *there* happen. Say "yes" to it ... let it unwind ... It's not our concern.

As Bhagavan Ramana says, "Why carry the baggage on your head to your own discomfort? Put it down on the train and let the train carry it." So, *now* we're putting it down ...

♥♥♥♥♥♥♥

By being in the Heart, there's nothing we need to do from Here. Our only "work" is to just *sit* Here in the Heart. Keep this as your foundation, as your base, and no longer let the body-mind and its experiences or thoughts be the basis of being.

Keep your choice, your vigilance to live this Truth ... be this Truth.

In this process, words are only being used to direct our attention towards the Silence, towards stillness. So, realize the Fullness in this Silence ... Realize the contentment ... the fulfillment ... the completeness that is Here in this Silence ... Nothing needs to be added, nothing needs to be taken away. It's all absolutely perfect. Realize this now as your own direct realization. Not as a philosophy *about* it, but imbibing of it, now, basking in it ...

♥♥♥♥♥♥♥

From Here, all the direction that the body-mind needs in day-to-day life is given ... So simple, so clear; no questions or doubts. Here in the Heart, we have never been touched by anything that the body-mind has been involved in. Already free ... already clear ... This is our True Nature. From Here, there is no past, no future, just the fresh moment of Now ... Now ... Feel the freshness ...

♥♥♥♥♥♥♥

In this stillness and silence, the total functioning of manifestation that is in charge of this body-mind in day-to-day life will occur naturally, like water flowing downhill. There's absolutely no effort on your part, it's already flowing in that direction.

There's only one thing to do. It's not really "doing," it's Being; just being right here in the Heart. The Self-Inquiry is then used like the light switch to bring us back into the light. If we have a tendency to re-identify with the body-mind, we use the Inquiry to return our attention back here into the Heart.

It's so simple. There's only one thing to do. Of course, the mind wants to do many things, make it very complicated, or say there's a whole lot more to do and distract us from the simplicity. But there's only one thing to do: just Be. Be here in the Heart. Just choose this. Say "Yes" to what Is.

Any separation from the Heart, from the Self, is felt as a contraction. So we know if we're straying; if it becomes difficult, an effort, or struggle, it's a clue. And we Inquire and we return to the Heart where everything flows …

Receive this message of Truth from one who is living from the Heart, and only sharing … just sharing.

♥♥♥♥♥♥

So, as we remain in this Stillness, in this Silence, we can now allow talking to occur from Here. If there are any questions, any sharing that wants to come forth from you, the sharing of your experience, or anything you would like to ask in this moment, just feel free to let it occur.

Participant: I have a question. Is it enough for me to be in the Heart and just say "Yes" to everything, or am I to discriminate along the lines of the "Real from the unreal?"

Elizabeth: The main thing here is, when we first receive something, it's important that we say "Yes" to it, *no matter what it is*, so there's no clouding of the issue. There's just complete clarity present. And then in that clarity the wisdom will be seen; the discrimination or the distinction or whatever it is to be seen will be seen. It's just a matter of priority here.

Otherwise, we're using the mind to discriminate and there will be a sense of right and wrong

It's just so *simple*; the mind makes it so complicated. And that's why we usually don't surrender to the Heart. The mind brings up fears – "I'm overwhelmed," "How am I going to handle this?" "How can I function with all these responsibilities?" or simply "I just can't do this anymore!" Then with all of this, we don't allow ourselves to merge with the Heart and we miss the opportunity.

Participant: It takes a lot of energy to worry about what to do.

Elizabeth: It sure does … *A lot* of energy. And, does this work?

Participant: Of course not!

Elizabeth: So we come to a place where we say, "It's time for me to do what actually works here." *And* it's simple. Initially, yes, there's an effort to remain in the Heart because our tendency is so strong to go "out there" into the conditioned mind. But that's just initially, in the beginning of the Inquiry process. And then as you continue the practice, abiding in the Peace of the Heart becomes easier and easier.

Next Participant: I'm curious about the process of "sitting in the Heart." I've never had any experience with this process until now and I don't know what to do when a situation comes up.

Elizabeth: What are you experiencing right now?

Participant: I'm feeling pretty quiet ...

Elizabeth: Does that feel good to you?

Participant: Yes. I feel peaceful.

Elizabeth: And is there any effort to feeling peaceful right now or is that just what's happening?

Participant: That's just what's happening.

Elizabeth: Yes. That's sitting in the Heart. It's what we *are*. It is our natural State. And usually, because we are so used to *doing* something, we literally separate from this to do something different. And then we get involved and totally forget this is here. So we make decisions based on this separation from the Heart – we make them from the mind, from the past, from what did or didn't work before, from worry, or whatever.

Does this work? Sometimes you win and sometimes you lose. And you suffer a lot. We have a choice to function from Here, from the Heart, where wisdom is, where paradoxically we are being directed from all the time. But we usually deny this direction, and go somewhere else. Now, here we are. The Heart, the

Awareness, *can* be the basis, the foundation from which you live your life. This *is* possible. It's not only possible, it is what's Real, what's True. Can you experience this right now with me? It's not what I'm speaking *of*, it's where I'm experiencing it *from* ...

♥♥♥♥♥♥

It's very practical. It can be used in our day-to-day life – while walking, talking, working, making love, or whatever.

Participant: So the experience of "living meditation" is living the Heart and knowing that *from* the Heart, we make our choices and decisions?

Elizabeth: Yes. Have you ever made a choice you really felt was right, even though maybe everyone else felt it was not right, and you couldn't even give a reason why? It was like, "This is just *right*, I can *feel* it." Well, that's the Heart speaking. That's the Heart directing.

Now ... just stay Here in the Heart.

Namasté!

That Which is Real

Following a guided meditation by Elizabeth ...

Participant: I just want to share two things that happened for me tonight. One is when you mentioned not "being the doer," I could just feel myself drop into the Heart, and a huge *load* came off of me. What actually is "the doer?"

Elizabeth: The doer is when you have left the Heart and returned to identifying with the body-mind as being the Self, as being who you think you are, which is not the Truth. Bhagavan Ramana says it this way: "Why leave the cool of the shade to go out into the sun to your own discomfort?"

Participant: I think I've actually been "the doer" since then. I've lost some of the lightness that I felt.

Elizabeth: So, from where is this doer arising? Just watch it. Look and see. What's really happening here? Face it, or look directly at it. *Really be aware of it!*

Anytime the "I" rises as the "doer," look it straight in the eye; not from the corner of your eye. Don't allow it to sneak in. Because we *know* it, we can *feel* it. It's like having an absolutely placid pool of water, such as here at the Center on our Reflection Lake on a calm day. You can be sitting there watching it being absolutely still; and then a fish will come up or the wind rises and causes this little ripple.

Feeling the rising of the "I" can also be compared to a spider feeling movement on its web. A spider can tell when anything is on its web; it's immediately aware of it.

It knows exactly where it is, and can go suddenly to it. We must *be* like that spider on the web, noticing immediately whatever is on the "web" of our consciousness, and immediately draw awareness to it. Not that we have to go there and get caught up in it, but to just be *aware*. This Awareness that is aware of "I," is "prior to" this "I," is *That Which Sees* it. From this perspective we are already free.

By giving our full attention to it, from the pure light of Awareness, it is exposed like photographic film exposed to light. It's *gone.*

That's our practice: no longer being at the effect of those things that come up in our lives ... But, rather, being Here, present, conscious, and alert to it. It *can't survive* in this Light! What we're actually doing here is exposing it and its illusory quality, revealing that it's not real, and the *Real* wins out every time.

♥♥♥♥♥♥

Participant: I now see that during your meditation, I was drawn into the Heart and felt a load released. And then, just as you said, I was unaware of it creeping back in until, all of a sudden, I realized that the heavy feeling had returned.

Elizabeth: Yes. This "load" gets removed by investigation, first by telling the truth about what we are experiencing right now. As soon as we notice that there's something here that's distracting us from the Heart, we ask "Who's having this experience?"

The answer can only be "I am."

This is the method for bringing it into our Awareness, into our attention, and taking full responsibility for it. *I'm* holding on to this distraction from the Heart. *I'm* doing it *to me.*

In the first part of the Inquiry we ask, "Where is it being felt in the body? ... What are the emotions? Who's having this experience? And we answer, "I am." Now we've got it in our Awareness. It's like grabbing hold of a "slippery eel" with "sandpaper gloves." It's in our clutches now, in our Awareness. And then with the "Who am I?" it dissolves. It fully brings it all into the Heart, and it's gone. It exposes it fully.

Our investigating into it is what will expose it fully and we'll be finished with it. This is the practice. This is *all* it is. Anything else is just a distraction from doing the practice in its simplicity.

Be *here* in the Heart now ...

♥♥♥♥♥♥♥

Participant: I am. What you're saying is so elegant, so simple, and so true. And, in some ways it is so *obvious.* So it's having the direct experience of, as you're putting it, of "investigating into the 'I,'" and learning how to experience it fully through Self-Inquiry?

Elizabeth: Yes. Then you're not going to be fooled any longer, because, you'll have the advantage of being in the Heart, fully and presently. We can look at it: what is it that's stopping me from being in the Heart?

Many times people come here, especially in our first programs, thinking they're going to get a good meditation technique, and they're going to *learn* something new to take home in order to finally awaken sometime in the future. It's actually living *from* the Heart, the Self, *now,* rather than learning some technique to take home with you to use in the hopes of one day *eventually* "making it."

Now is the time! Be here and now in the I AM! Awake and present in the Heart! And then live *from* That. That's the practice of *Living from the Heart*, the Self. The practice isn't really "practice," it's *being* the true, pure Self.

Take the time now to create your intention: "Okay, it's time. It's time for me to *be* That NOW," not look for it sometime in the future. For that is what's occurring Here and Now. Feel this Now ...

♥♥♥♥♥♥

Next Participant: I want to go back to what you were saying. That is so true, because since returning home from the Retreat Center, I now stay with the experience of Living from the Heart. It's just amazing what a difference it makes to directly experience that for myself; it's not just some concept. And then when something comes up I just clear it. I continue to *sit* here in the Heart. I made up my mind to do the one-hour meditation in the morning and an hour at night, and keep the Heart Times, and I just told myself, "This is what I'm going to do. I will just get up earlier, and that's what I will do." And I'm now successfully doing that. What I'm finding in these last few weeks is that I only average about four hours of sleep a night and I still feel *great* every day!

Elizabeth: Yes, that's it! Ordinarily we have dreams in order to unwind all of whatever it is that we didn't complete for the day, and then we might have three or four hours of deep dreamless sleep. The next part of the time period is the resistance to waking up. We dream, and the mind is continually trying to *stay* asleep so we won't have to wake up and carry on with whatever it is that we're resisting in our day-to-day life. So when we are meditating, as you are in the evening before you go to sleep, that will *unwind* and empty the mind. That's taking responsibility for that, ahead of time, so that you can move right into dreamless sleep. Then waking up becomes very easy – you're refreshed.

When you take the time to meditate, to start your day off in the Heart, you won't be so involved in the mind's activities of the day.

Your practice and your process is speeding up because you're unwinding the mind. It would otherwise continue to fight and keep you out of the Heart. So the commitment you've made is very powerful. I'm glad to hear it. At some point in our practice here in AHAM, it's very clear to all of us – whether it's in the beginning, or the middle, or near the end – that it's entirely up to each one of us. It dawns on us all of a sudden that if we *really do* apply ourselves, if we *really are* vigilant with this practice, we are able to *Live from the Heart*. When we finally get this, and we really start applying ourselves to practicing the Self-Inquiry in our lives, then it's just amazing what begins to occur.

It's good if we get it closer to the beginning so we can benefit much quicker. But that's okay; wherever you are is wherever you are. If you haven't fully started already, start now. Be here now. Apply yourself – that's all that it takes.

There are those who *are truly committed* and who are vigilant to remain in the Heart; this is what we call a "Buddha Field." This is created from those who are living and abiding the Heart in Conscious Company, which is lending to the transformational quality for everyone present in this company. Persons coming for the first time are receiving this as their initial experience. So as long as you're receptive, willing and open to it, it just happens. You come right into it.

Next Participant: I just want to let you know how I'm doing. The mind makes me want to break the commitment to living this Teaching. It's driving me crazy, you know what I mean?

Elizabeth: Yes, I do. There are certain conditioned patterns that stay hidden from us. They seem to be very deeply rooted, that are like saboteurs preventing us from remaining in the Heart. And now these mind patterns, this conditioning is bringing up ... "NO, you don't deserve it, you don't deserve being free." The mind is what's dictating, rather than you as the Heart.

Begin to look at those conditioned patterns that are keeping you from being exactly where you want to be. Seeing them from the Heart, you burn them out, you clear them out of the space. You've got what it takes, and all the right ingredients.

In directly confronting it, the mind is already throwing up its strategies and games to keep you from even participating in and continuing in your commitment. Just by your staying with your commitment and continuing to stay with your practice, you *can* keep an upper hand. Stand up to it. Stand up to the mind! The power of the Self, the Heart, is present. But without this continued commitment we end up giving in. Stay with your practice.

As soon as we see this, we stand up to what's not real from the Prior Awareness. We let it be known who's *really* in charge here. It's like being a parent. There are a lot of times we can get pulled in and our kids wrap us around their little finger. And that kind of thing – we know as a parent – cannot go on. It is not appropriate, and in the long run it's not good for the child. It's exactly the same with the mind. For so long we have let it run the show. Now it must be disciplined and must know who's in charge.

When we first start taking back that responsibility of being the one in charge, it's going to resist just like a child would. It will put up a *good* fight. But you don't give in. See how there are a lot of parallels here.

We're coming to the end of tonight's Heart Line time together, but the Heart line itself continues; that's the beauty of it. We're *never* alone; the room is *full.* It's so beautiful, so powerful ... the networking that we have now, in Conscious Company. The Buddha Field is getting so *big* ... *so full!* We can enjoy this all the time, just connecting, linking in, and being together, in the Heart.

Namasté!

Get Behind the Mind

Following a guided meditation by Elizabeth ...

Participant: I've got a question. When you say to follow the "I" into the Heart, what does that mean? I keep going down to the stomach.

Elizabeth: It's not a visual process. It doesn't really have anything to do with the body.

Participant: So it's actually not a feeling?

Elizabeth: Yes, it is a feeling, but it's not located in the body. We can locate what people talk about as the heart center in the body, but we are not talking about that when we talk about the "Heart." The Heart includes something much bigger than that.

Experience this now ... You exist. You are conscious. Right now, isn't there a distinct feeling of "I" as *existence* right now?

Participant: Yes.

Elizabeth: That is the feeling of "I." Who can say "I" for you? Only you can. No one else can say that for you. So, you see, it is a distinct feeling. This "I-feeling," that is what you get in touch with. And as you keep feeling that "I," it will automatically pull your attention into the Source. It's not something *you* have to do. All you have to do is feel the "I" and it draws your attention naturally into the Source. Many people think this practice is something that you have to *do*. Well, yes you do have to follow the step-by-step process,

Living the Truth

Following a guided meditation by Elizabeth ...

Participant: I appreciate the meditation very much. I felt a stillness and also a clearing about something that had been going over and over in my head all week. It seems to be clearing, so thank you very much.

Elizabeth: Yes. It's a very simple but very powerful process. It's like pouring wonderful fresh water into a stagnant area, whether it's a stream or a pool, or a bucket of water. Whatever is in there that isn't clear and pure, removes itself in the presence of what is pure.

Participant: There's a deep relaxation ... something very special.

Elizabeth: The body responds to that Presence that we are. It's not natural for the body to be tight, or the mind to be racing. That isn't what's natural, even though that often seems to be the habitual reaction that the body-mind has to things around us. But once we have this connection with our true Self and we choose freedom, choose happiness, choose Self above all else, then we remember what's natural again, and what's not natural becomes very evident. Instead of choosing to remain upset, reacting to things, or being uptight, we are bringing our attention back to the Source. So our attention is on Peace, and Lightness, Creativity, Spontaneity – all the things that feel good, natural and real.

It's all about being real. No longer having to wear masks and costumes, and being stuck there. Oh yes, we do have to continue playing the roles. Be sure we, "Play the roles, don't be the roles." Don't forget who you are that is playing this role. Play it as if you were an actor or actress on a stage. Give yourself fully to it, but don't be it. "God is playing all the roles." Accept that, and accept whatever God wants to play in this moment.

The body-mind is so clearly second to what's real. We get it that it's just an instrument for the Heart, for what's real. It's not *what* I am, or *who* I am. Who I am and what I am is the Stillness, is the Silence.

Be this now ...

♥♥♥♥♥♥

That which Is, the Pure Awareness, is going on between the words, between the movement of thought or the movement of the body. Pure Awareness is what is still and present eternally. It is always awake, always aware, always present. Pure Awareness is entirely conscious of what's occurring in the moment. When we can come from That, in every moment, we don't miss a thing. We catch what's going on, and are guided wisely from the Heart for the good of all concerned. We are choosing from the perspective of the Whole and no longer from an individual "piece."

Many of us are into problem-solving and trying to figure it all out, rather than just going into the Heart and seeing what's so. It is all there. The wisdom and the insights are there. Following these insights may be scary because maybe you may not have followed the Heart before, and you don't know what's next. But somehow intuitively we know it's real, we know it is what is true for us. We don't compromise that, and we follow that. It will give us the strength to go through the changes that we need to go through to complete what we're here to complete.

So it makes life very simple when we come from the Heart in our day-to-day lives. Initially it makes for a little adjustment, but after a while everything falls into place. It is just right and true. Feel this simplicity ... from the Heart's perspective ...

♥♥♥♥♥♥

Next Participant: I have a question about motives when coming from the Heart. That seems to be a real focal point that my life has come to, what I do in my engagements with people, especially in regards to money. It's difficult to be a sales person without a motive. I was wondering if Ramana has ever spoken about that, because everybody has to make money. It doesn't necessarily have to be in sales. I would agree with that. But it seems like living from the Heart would be living without a motive.

Elizabeth: Well, the Heart consciously directs us into what we need to do. The important thing with regard to money is that we see that it's not first cause, it's second cause. It's not what we primarily look for in regards to what we're doing, whatever that may be. If our job is sales, for example, we should look at what is our purpose. What are we *giving* to life in this moment in this particular job, in this particular venture? And in looking at what we're giving to life, what is the service that we're rendering here? Our motive isn't money, it's *service*.

Not that money doesn't come out of that, it certainly does. I was in sales for a number of years, radio advertising, which is a very highly competitive business. Whenever I went in to visit a client I wouldn't try to make the quota that day, or try to make a sale. I would find out what I could do right now to serve them; what were their needs, and how to serve them in that moment. And, as it turned out, I became one of the best sales people on staff at the best radio station in that area at the time. So I'm speaking from experience. It was a nice surprise for me to see such a simple principle at work. I was so grateful to have had a way to access the creative abilities that come from Living in the Heart.

I was practicing the Inquiry process at that time, which naturally created my coming from the Heart when I was with clients. I was there for them, and what I could do *to serve them*. The ideas came forth, and the creativity was there, and the sales came easily.

The motive isn't to make money. The motive is to serve, and that's giving. So, would we call that a motive? I don't know. Does that make any sense?

Participant: Yes. I think I just have to keep investigating, that's all. I'm sure it's true, but I have to experience it myself. But I hear what you're saying.

Elizabeth: Yes. It's a different approach. It's a different angle to look at and to see what's going on. I used to do consulting. I had my own consulting business. I would go into a business and look at their problems. I discussed with the owners what their purpose was in the beginning, when they initially began the business. It was almost always to serve. And then after awhile their purpose seemed to change to making money. They had lost their original purpose, which was basically to serve.

So we got back to that, just that simple thing: "What is your purpose here? What are you doing here? What are you giving to the community or to your clients?" And they'd say, "Well gosh, I haven't thought about that since I first began this." And so we got back into that and then everything started working out from there. It's amazing. So, as you look at your job and you look at what you're doing, and what you're selling, look at your purpose, and what is important for serving each client.

After being in sales for a while, I realized that this was my way to connect with people in the Heart. So even though our friendship may have been based on a very mundane thing such as figuring out what their advertising scheme is, or in getting their business problems solved, we were still able to be in the Heart together. I was able to share that with them.

I feel that is one of the most important things we can share with each other. So my purpose escalated from selling and giving a service and creative ideas to my client, to sharing the Heart together. That was the highest purpose I could find in our relationship together.

The key here is to be able to remain in the Heart with eyes open, throughout the day, in your day-to-day life. And that's a challenge – keeping that connection and not being pulled out and distracted.

"Exclusive contemplation of the Heart is inclusive of everything else." Realize this for yourself ...

♥♥♥♥♥♥

Giving our attention to the Heart may seem as though all our responsibilities get left behind. But exclusive attention on the Heart is *inclusive* of everything else. We become more aware, more conscious and more creative, because we're not limiting ourselves in any way. We're not missing things. We're picking up on things. It actually works much better.

Participant: So then would you say that transformation is the result of this entire process?

Elizabeth: Yes, a radical transformation is what occurs when you're able to make that 180-degree shift in awareness, from being at the effect of things coming and going in your life, to being That which is prior to it, behind all that's coming and going. You're now able to function consciously in life. Things go on, responsibilities are taken. Actually you're able to be more efficient and more creative because you're not stuck in any limitations of fear or desires that arise. This is the complete transformation. This is *Living* from the Heart.

Namasté.

Let the Heart Conduct
Your Life

Following is a guided meditation by Elizabeth:

Participant: What I've been experiencing for the past couple of months is a sensation of a strong "sucking" feeling when I come into the "I" or feeling the "I," as I'm moving through that. And there's also some vertigo along with that, like feeling topsy-turvy. There's been a bit of not wanting to completely let go into that, because it feels so odd. It's like being on a boat that's rocking, flipping. And then as I move through it, I feel the stillness. My question is whether you have had any experience, or any kind of insight about those feelings where it feels like vertigo. It's like the energy's flipping around.

Elizabeth: Just understand, all of that is going on in the body. You are Here as the Prior Awareness, seeing it as there, going on in the body. So remember to just stay *Here*, seeing it going on *there*, in the body. Then, whatever is going on ... is whatever is going on. It's OK. You're accepting of it. Stay Here, seeing it there, and you are free.

This Awareness is the Heart. It is *prior* or back behind it all. It is where everything rises out of and everything returns. So, that sensation is occurring in the body, *not to you*, the one who is aware of it. Be as this Prior Awareness now ...

♥♥♥♥♥♥

Participant: And when I come into this Prior Awareness and stay with it, the body sensations will intensify before it passes on?

Elizabeth: Whether it intensifies or not, you're still *Here*. So it doesn't really matter. That's very important to see, otherwise we won't allow it to go all the way through. We'll get caught up in the sensational experience of it. And the experience isn't *it*. You're still the Awareness of whatever experience or sensation is occurring in the body.

As we truly dedicate our attention to abiding in the Heart, these kinds of things may occur in the body. It's just a clearing process. Be sure that you don't get caught and make that real. It's just what's going on in the moment.

Next Participant: Elizabeth, I've been noticing today that while I'm in the Heart, I feel almost detached. I was doing my job today and enjoying everything. I was in my office, I was talking to the people there on my job, but it was almost as if I wasn't really there. And I'm wondering, is this just a feeling that the mind has that's going on … a judgment … that I feel detached?

I've been feeling as though I never left the Center since I've come back from the weekend. When I'm in the Heart, it's just a weird feeling of detachment. Maybe it's just me. Maybe that's it.

Elizabeth: Yes. That *is* you, that's the *true* you. That is *being in* the Self, in the Heart. Obviously it's not something that you've had come up before. But it's really what is. It's just what's going on naturally.

We may have been so identified with the body-mind, thinking that the body-mind is who we are. And we lose track of that Awareness that is aware of all this that is going on. And now you're abiding in the Heart, just watching it all happening. Now stay right *Here*.

Participant: Yes. I think that was it. That's exactly how I was feeling. I was watching the world go on around me. And *I* put that title on it of being "weird."

Elizabeth: Yes. See that's what the conditioned mind will throw up and say, "This isn't normal. This isn't real. Go back to where you were before. That's what you're accustomed to." But get the Truth, right here and now: that this is just the way it is, when you're living in and from the Heart. And this way, you're *not* at the effect of what's going on in the body-mind. You said things still went on, and you were not at the effect?

Participant: Yes. There was lots of upset in the office. But I wasn't in it. And they were looking at me like I was bizarre because I wasn't involved in it.

Elizabeth: Right, that's the natural state. We've all heard the term, "Let go and let God," for so long in our upbringing with what we received in our church or synagogue. "Let go and let God." What does that really mean? Well *this* is what it means. Let go into your true Being, into what *is* ... before anything else can be ... which is the Truth of who we are. And then let God run your life. Let the Heart run your life. Let it conduct the symphony. Just relax into it all ...

♥♥♥ ♥ ♥♥♥

Next Participant: Let's go back to what you said earlier. How can you be certain whether something that's going on in the body is OK, or whether it needs attention? How can you tell the difference?

Elizabeth: You mean as far as the body needing medical attention?

Participant: Yes, something like that. For instance, I was dizzy recently, and I thought it was my eye glasses. But I'm not too sure. I wasn't sure whether I needed to do something for my body, like maybe eat something, or whether some metaphysical experience was going on.

Elizabeth: I understand what you're saying. Well, in that case you just tune in and see. First do the Inquiry with it so that you're *Here* in the Heart with it, and it'll eventually subside. If it doesn't, then there may be something physical that needs to be attended to. You just have to take it one step at a time and use the process of elimination.

You don't want to be irresponsible if there is something physically wrong going on. It doesn't hurt to get it checked out. The main thing is to be *Here* in the Heart while it's going on *there* in the body, no matter what's going on. The wisdom comes from our being *Here*. Like you said, you felt like you needed to have something to eat. Go ahead and eat something. And then if there's still the dizziness, go to something else. The main thing is you're in the Heart with it.

Next Participant: When I'm in a relationship with someone, why does it seem like it doesn't really work psychologically?

Elizabeth: You mean you get pulled into the relationship? Is that what you mean?

Participant: Yes.

Elizabeth: Are you abiding *Here* in the Heart while you're in relationship with this person? Are you watching whatever is going on as "there" in the body-mind: the emotions and sensations?

Participant: Yes, I am.

Elizabeth: OK. So what part of it doesn't seem to work then?

Participant: I guess the trust.

Elizabeth: The trust? OK, the trust of the person, or the trust of being able to stay in the Heart? Which one?

Participant: I guess trust of the other person.

Elizabeth: So in the body-mind there is a sense of not trusting. Have there been occasions in the past, where you found out that you couldn't trust the person?

Participant: Oh yes!

Elizabeth: So that's a record or a pattern that you have in the body-mind. To begin to clear this you tell the truth … "OK, I see a lack of trust is here in relationships." Be with the experience that comes with this … then ask yourself, "When was the time I had this experience?" Let a scene come up and find out who is there and what is going on … And allow whatever is coming up to be revealed, to come up … And then do Inquiry. Who's experiencing this? … I AM … Who am I? … Feel "I-I-I" … Follow "I-I-I" … into the Source … into the Heart …

♥♥♥♥♥♥

This is an intentional way to clear out those patterns, because that's what's causing the distrust – the very pattern itself. It's not the person; it's the pattern in you that keeps coming up when you're around that person.

This is what we at AHAM call "working on ourselves." Where we intentionally work on areas just like this, where we finally take a stand to get clear of this, once and for all. But, before you go into the clearing, first realize, "I'm *Here* and it's *there*." Whatever you are aware of, it's not you. It's only something that's recorded in the body-mind, in that configuration *there*. It's not you. Just let it come up. Let the scene from the past come up, any scene. It's a very focused way to clear out whatever might be there. And then, after Inquiring, "Who is seeing this?" and seeing "I" am, and Inquiring, "Who am I?" you get back prior to the body-mind and the sense of distrust is totally released. Then you'll find that trust will just naturally be there. Feel this now …

The beauty of this teaching is that this work is being conducted *by* the Heart, not *toward* the Heart. So anytime we are working on those areas conditioned in the body-mind, *first* make sure that we're *Here* – already present in the Heart. And then allow whatever is *there* that needs to be cleared in the body-mind, to occur *from* the Heart. So then our spiritual work is being conducted *by* the Heart, not *toward* the Heart. It's not, "I'm going to clear this situation to finally be in the Heart." It is "I'm in the Heart *now*." *Then* look and see what situation needs clearing and focus the Light of Awareness on it, like shining a bright light into a dark area. And in the very presence of this Light it gets cleared out naturally.

An important element in this teaching is telling your self the truth. That's a major step in the right direction, when we admit to ourselves what's *really* going on in the moment, and stop fooling ourselves about it. Then, from here, use the Inquiry to clear it. Because whatever is going on in our world of experience is really something that is going on in us, something in the body-mind that needs to be looked at and cleared.

Next Participant: Quite often habit patterns take over and I forget, and then the sense of a separate self arises again. I wonder if it's just a matter of practice and it will keep bringing me back to the Heart, and that with time and practice the false sense of self will just subside.

Elizabeth: Yes, it is most definitely in the practice, as we remain in the true Self. And whatever comes up that isn't the Self is quite obvious. It feels like a contraction, or a tightness, a tension, which feels distinctly different. Once you've had the experience of the Self or the Heart, you can make that distinction between what's Real and what is not Real. It is just a matter of continuing to keep that agreement, that commitment to stay in the Self, and using the Inquiry if you find your attention is drifting outward.

Also, one of the things we've found in our sharing the Teaching here, and that I have seen in my working with people over the years, is that there are conditioned tendencies and patterns we are not even aware of, that are pulling our attention outward, away from the Heart.

Maintaining commitment to your spiritual work gives you the ability to live easily and effectively in the world. You are able to shine the Light on those areas that need conscious understanding, very distinctly, very directly. That is really "working on our selves" as I was speaking of earlier. Eventually the distractions of the world will not be coming up quite so often, because we've cleared out the negative and limiting patterns.

It is easier if you don't have to be all alone in the practice, especially when you get to the place of the final merging with the Self. Often there are some very subtle areas that block the way or distract and detour us from our final goal. It's important to be in Conscious Company, being present with those already living the Heart, awake and alive. You can ask questions and receive the truth *directly*, at the right time, so that you're not distracted whatsoever. It's a pure focus the entire time. Right now, are you in the Self?

Participant: Yes ... it's very peaceful and spacious.

♥♥♥♥♥♥♥

Next Participant: I'm so grateful for all the questions and all the comments, because it's right on target with what's coming up for me. These attachments and habits of the body-mind just seem to keep coming up in the course of daily living. Remaining in the Heart and watching it, I am able to be aware of these patterns that come up. I see how the mind pops up and says, "Well, I'm going to *do* this clearing. I'm going to *do* this Inquiry." And I see all of that as just another one of those patterns of "doing." The words, "The Heart *conducts* the clearing" are strong in assuring me that there's really no "doing" required. Things still come up, and yet the Heart *is* clearing it. And there's no "doing" involved.

Elizabeth: Yes, that's correct. And as the time progresses and as you continue to stay in that commitment of *Being in* the Self not *doing* it, then whatever comes up is dissolved very quickly. It's much easier this way. For some people it occurs almost automatically.

When allowing the Heart to conduct the clearing, you just zip right through it, because you're *not* going *there*.

You're not feeding the negative patterns with your attention. You're just allowing them to occur and be *naturally* dissolved *from* the Heart. This makes life a lot easier. Remember there will always be something coming up in the body-mind, to whatever degree or intensity you give your attention to it. It's been a long time that we've collected these conditioned patterns by identifying with it, thinking that it's "me." So it's no different than if you were on a health program, and your body started detoxing, removing all the poisons. It takes a while for it all to be removed from the body. It's no different here. And when you're sitting in the Heart, you're not collecting any additional "poison" or patterns to have to be cleared later. So there is an end to it, right *now!*

The main thing is that we don't have to *jump in* to clear it. We stay right *Here* in the Heart, already free, already clear. Feel this now …

♥♥♥♥♥♥

Next Participant: Elizabeth, I've been experiencing a lot of resistance in meditating, because I've been really identifying with emotional pain. It's been very difficult to meditate, very difficult even to read the literature. There is this big block going on, and the harder I try, the more resistance comes up. Recently I said to myself, "Forget this! I'm not going to try anymore. So is that a good thing, to drop *trying* to meditate. Or is that just the mind wanting to take over and have its way?

Elizabeth: If you are *trying* to meditate, and *trying* to be in the Heart, obviously there is a "doer" there. And there is an "I" that thinks it is already separate from the heart. So around and around in the circle you go, and tighter and tighter is the contraction. It's like the knot gets tighter and tighter, rather than getting loosened. So if you just stop *trying*, stop *doing* and just rest, just *sit* or abide in what's already presently going on, you are already *Here*. But if there's any "trying," then obviously there is an assumption that you are separate from the Heart. And you're going further and further away from It. When you stop trying, what is already *Here* is allowed to come forward. It now has the space to come forward.

Do you hear that?

Participant: Could you clarify that a bit?

Elizabeth: When the "trying" and "doing" come up, make sure you're *Here* and it's *there*. Just ask yourself "Who is seeing and experiencing this?" The answer is … "I AM" … Feel this "I AM" …

Notice from this perspective that "I AM" *Here,* and the "trying" and "doing" is *there"* Be *Here* seeing your experience is *there*, in the body-mind. From *Here* you are already out … you are already free. See that it is all merely thought. Who is thinking all of that? … I AM … Remain *Here* in the Self, the Heart, aware of it all and you are no longer affected by *any* of it.

Namasté!

*Living
the
Teaching*

We all have to return to our source. Every human being is seeking his source and must one day come to it. We came from the Within; we have gone outward and now we must turn inward. What is meditation? It is our natural Self. We have covered ourselves over with thoughts and passions. To throw them off we must concentrate on one thought: the Self.

The Self is like a powerful magnet hidden within us. It draws us gradually to Itself, though we imagine we are going to It of our own accord. When we are near enough, It puts an end to our other activities, makes us still, and then swallows up our own personal current. It overwhelms the intellect and floods the whole being. We think we are meditating upon It and developing towards It, whereas the truth is, that we are like iron-filings and It is the Self-magnet that is pulling us towards Itself. Thus the process of finding Self is a form of divine magnetism.

> Bhagavan Sri Ramana Maharshi
> *Conscious Immortality*
> by Paul Brunton and Munagala Venkataramiah
> Sri Ramanasramam, Tiruvannamalai,
> South India, 1984.

The Heart Cave Meditation

Whenever the mind is actively distracting your attention away from the Heart, the True Self Nature that you are, use this simple process.

The words in bold in this meditation are from Bhagavan Ramana with some additions to guide the meditation experience. These words reflect the entire teaching of Self Inquiry. It has been created into a meditation process for an awakening of this Truth to be fully experienced.

To begin the process, come into a comfortable position in your chair ... now read over the first paragraph ... slowly ... and feel attention being drawn into this Truth ...

... *"In the Interior of the Heart Cave, The Lord God Alone Abides with Direct Immediacy as I-I-I"* ...

Feel these words ... deeply accepting this Truth ...

♥♥♥♥♥♥♥

... *"Enter into this Heart Cave with Questing Mind"* ...

To enter into this Heart Cave of your True Being, ask yourself ... "Who am I?" ...

Feel and follow I – I – I ...

♥♥♥♥♥♥♥

... *"Diving Deep Within"* ...

... feel and follow this I-I-I-feeling with your entire attention, diving deep within, letting everything else go ...

♥♥♥♥♥♥♥

... *"Controlling the Breath"* ...

There is no need for effort in controlling the breath. From the previous steps, you have realized the Source of breath, the Pure Awareness, the Heart ... from Here, Breathless Awareness happens naturally.

Let go into this Breathless Awareness ... for as long as you wish ...

♥♥♥♥♥♥♥

At this time, the ego/mind's strategies of separation from one's True Nature are being dissolved into the Heart effortlessly. So, if you can remain as this Breathless, Thoughtless Awareness it is extremely beneficial for your spiritual practice.

Then, the final paragraph is what you live, moment-to-moment in your life as you continue to remain in the Heart Cave through practicing this meditation process.

... *Happily abide Herein, Remaining Light, Natural and Free* ...

♥♥♥♥♥♥♥

In the Interior of the Heart Cave [Of Your Being]
The Lord God Alone Abides
With Direct Immediacy
As I-I-I ...

Enter into this Heart Cave
With Questing Mind ... "Who Am I?"
Diving Deep Within ... Feel and Follow I-I-I
Controlling the Breath ... Breathless Awareness

NOW, Happily Abide Herein ...
Remaining Light, Natural and Free ...

♥♥♥♥♥♥♥

Heart-felt Sharing

The following writings are from graduates of AHAM's programs who are living from the Heart.

I can remember kneeling in the church pew when I was very young and feeling something was missing. Praying to God didn't feel right to me. Over the years I came to believe there was a higher power greater than myself and I thought it was outside of me. I saw it in the beauty of nature around me. I saw it in the animals in my care. I saw it in how everything is interrelated. I found a place at times within myself to go to when in pain physically or emotionally – where I was "here" but "not here," where the pain was gone, where my mind would be still, where I could sleep – a place I could not explain. Little did I know ...

I found that "place" again after coming to AHAM. Self-inquiry led me to that place within, the Self, the Truth, where the *real* me is. Who am I? What a relief to no longer have to define myself – that place within is who I am, nothing else.

– Lucy Segerson

♥♥♥♥♥♥

I discovered AHAM on the Internet while looking for books on Advaita Vedanta. I must have been divinely guided. I began the Power of Awareness (POA) training in August 2003 and since then there has been no turning back. While the path has not been easy (so sayeth the mind), it has been consistently rewarding. The Intensive Self-Inquiry Training (I SIT) in November of 2003 added depth to the feeling of I AM. Since Neutralizing Negative Past (NNP) this year, I AM has deepened much more. This was my favorite course with AHAM thus far. I like how it entwines itself with POA and I SIT. As I take responsibility for my life and the events in it, I move closer to being at the cause of life rather than at its effect, and there is less suffering and less of one who suffers. The correspondence courses have been brilliant and I don't think I would have continued in the practice of the Presence without them – they are essential.

– David Karlovich

♥♥♥♥♥♥

Time and Time again, I cried out in anguish to God to free me from the pain of separation. I felt so empty and lonely even though there was much that seemingly occupied my time and life. Always I craved for fulfillment and freedom.

Now there is light where there was darkness; freedom where there was bondage; love where there was fear and self-loathing, and peace where there was despair.

How do I ever show my love and gratitude? In humility, I dedicate this remaining life to serving this Highest Purpose and hopefully others will find the same joy and freedom through that service.

– Charlotte Twardokus

♥♥♥♥♥♥

Through Self-Inquiry and other transformational processes, the melodrama of living life on lifes's terms "feels to be playing itself out," meaning it's playing less of a role because I am at less at effect of persons, places and things in living my life today. The intense loneliness and separation experienced in active addiction is non-existent, for it only resulted from my ignorance in being identified with the conditioned limitations of the mind, as opposed to living in the Reality of my own Being. AHAM's teaching is the vehicle that encourages and empowers me to determine, for myself, that the detrimental effects of drug addiction and all other forms of limitation stem from the primary addiction to being identified with the body-mind, manifesting as conditioned patters of thought. In Truth, I am not that! The implementation of the AHAM 10 Conscious Principles within the Sponsorship Program allows me to see the falsity of all self-held beliefs and concepts that perpetuate the addiction to conditioned patterns of thought.

- Ed Segerson

♥♥♥♥♥♥

Little did I know nine years ago when I took my first program, "Discover Meditation," I would be in the role(s) I am now playing with AHAM and in all areas of my life. I thought I was coming to the AHAM Center to learn how to meditate, not knowing that my life would be completely transformed in one incredible weekend. Through the past nine years of my association with AHAM I have experienced a blossoming into the One I had been searching for just in the process of life itself. I now realize that the One has always been here … "She" just needed a little uncovering and "buffing!" Thank you Ramana and Elizabeth for the gift of Me. Truly this is the gift that keeps giving and giving!

– Michele Bordelon

♥♥♥♥♥♥

Words are limited by their form and can't describe the bliss of pure oneness of Self. Before I participated in AHAM's programs my life was somewhat chaotic, with an endless series of dramas speckled by intermittent glimpses of peace and joy. Since childhood, listening to the words of Jesus, and bringing them into me to make sense within me, I've recognized that I am God's creation and within me, in the still, silent Heart lies the answer to all my questions.

The AHAM programs I have participated in have been milestones in this transformational process. It has carried me through all the major crises I have ever had, completing them and freeing me. These milestones are celebrations along the path of learning to be fully present in each moment. The day-to-day, moment-to-moment practice of giving attention only to the authentic Self has been possible only through the support, communion and guidance of Consciousness Itself.

– Donna Hale

It Is really beyond words what the realization of the true "Self" is. Words are merely ideas or concepts and there are no words to adequately express the gratitude for the first hand experience of being directed to the home within. The treasure was there all along and it was hidden without my knowledge of it. What a magical moment it is and still even remains. I don't have to go anywhere – it is already here. The experience felt in awakening to the true "Being," the true "Self" cannot be comprehended but must be discovered first hand – it is wordless, beyond words. All just melts in the silence … there are no thoughts … stillness permeates … the heart radiance is expressed and shared … Oneness is experienced … It grows larger with each Being who realize the nature of one's true "Being." I can recall numerous times when I have become speechless, and any questions I did have melted away instantly in the bliss of the silence as I redirected attention to the "I AM." The silence is so profound, incredible, magical, and unbelievable.

– Nadine Antos

♥♥♥♥♥♥♥

I am experiencing a peace that I did not imagine was possible. It is because you have shared the teachings of Sri Bhagavan Ramana Maharshi in a manner that is practical, providing me with tools to use moment-to-moment. Because body-mind identification appeared to be the very essence of what I had chosen as my life's work, which is racial justice, this body-mind created all forms of resistance to the teaching. Yet, the heart-resonance is so strong in AHAM and in its conscious curriculum that the resistance thrown up by this body-mind melts in the fire of the heart. Self-Inquiry and the conscious tools that have come through you have strengthened attention to the Heart and weakened identification with the world. Through your guidance I know what it is to be in the world but not of the world.

– Adjoa Aiyetoro

♥♥♥♥♥♥♥

♥♥♥♥♥♥

Self-Inquiry Process

The following step-by-step Self-Inquiry Process is experienced in the "Intensive Self-Inquiry Series Program (I SIT)" at AHAM. A recorded guided meditation is also available to assist your practice.

We have found that having assistance in fully experiencing this process is essential, so that it doesn't become a mental process. Therefore, we encourage you to participate in the above-mentioned program to be assured of proper instruction and guidance.

Check In. Where am I now?

Wherever you are, whomever you're with, whatever you're doing in your active lifestyle, or while sitting in meditation, "check in" to see if you are presently "Sitting peacefully in the Heart of Being, in the prior Awareness of the Self; abiding in the Here and Now."

Or, is your attention elsewhere, distracted by thoughts going on in the mind about your life situation, i.e., some present concern, or some past event, or a future anticipation or expectation?

Ask yourself, *"Where am I now?"*

♥♥♥♥♥♥

What am I experiencing right now?

If you see that you are "Sitting still in the Heart," then just remain there. But if you see that you have been distracted, pulled out of the NOW, then be aware of exactly what you are experiencing.

Ask yourself: *"What am I experiencing, right now?"*

♥♥♥♥♥♥♥

First, notice the experience that is occurring in the body. This will take you out of your ego-mind that distracts you by trying to figure "it" out, make "it" reasonable or try to "fix it" in some way. Then, once you have the location of the experience in the body, you see what emotions are present and finally what thoughts are present. Let the experience be as it is.

Self-Inquiry Questions

Get the entire experience in your awareness. Ask yourself, *"Who is experiencing this?"*

The obvious answer, "I" am.

Pause here and *Feel I-AM.*

♥♥♥♥♥♥♥

Recognize "I AM *Here,* accepting what's *there."*

♥♥♥♥♥♥♥

Ask yourself: *"Who am I?"*

Feel and follow "I-I-I."

♥♥♥♥♥♥♥

Let go into the inward flow of Consciousness ...

It will magnetically draw your attention into the prior Pure Awareness, the Heart, the Self ... into Pure Being, the One Reality.

♥♥♥♥♥♥♥

Rest in the Prior Awareness, in Pure Being

Thoughts and experiences will come and go; just observe them in the body-mind. But you remain *Here* ... in the Now Presence ... in this Prior Awareness ... and don't go *there*.

♥♥♥♥♥♥♥

All you need to know in the moment will be revealed from the Wisdom of the True Self, and not from the conditioned and limited past of the body-mind.

This is Living Free, Happy, Contented ... at Peace ... abiding in the Freshness of NOW.

♥♥♥♥♥♥

I AM THAT ...

I AM is not a thought.
It is my Infinite and Eternal Self.
Use it like a "polishing cloth"
to clean the mirror of mind,
Asking myself here and now ...
"Who's feeling this present experience?"
I AM ...

Feel ... *I AM* ...
Feeling *I AM*, the Heart Shines.
There is no feeling of "I" and "mine."
There is only *I AM* ...
The accumulation of thought
As past, present and future...
Is the "I-am-the-body" thought.
Asking myself here and now ...
"Who am I?" ...

Feel "I-I-I" ... this Pure Awareness only ...
The "I-thought" is withdrawn into the Heart
And, past-present-future are gone ...
There is only the "I-I Awareness" ...
Only *Pure I AM* ... and
I AM THAT.

♥▾♥♥♥♥▾

That Which Sees

The first Western devotee of Sri Bhagavan, Frank Humphreys, came to Him in 1911 when He was living up on the Hill Arunachala, at Virupaksha Cave. Bhagavan shared this wisdom with him at that time.

Bhagavan: I have given you this teaching in the same words as the Master gives to intimate *chelas* [disciples]. From now onwards, let your thought in meditation be not on the act of seeing, nor on what you see, but immovably on "That Which Sees."

The phenomena we see are curious and surprising - but the most marvelous of all, we do not realize, and that is the one and only one illimitable force which is responsible for *all the phenomena we see; and the act of seeing them.*

Do not fix your attention on all these changing things of life, death and phenomena. Do not think of even the actual act of seeing or perceiving them, but only of that which sees all these things - that which is responsible for it all. This will seem nearly impossible at first, but by degrees the result will be felt ... keep the mind unshakably fixed on That Which Sees.

*Glimpses of the Life and Teachings of
Sri Ramana Maharshi*
As described by Frank H. Humphreys
Sri Ramanasramam, Tiruvannamalai, South India, 1999.

Being in
Conscious
Company

What is the essential nature of "upadesa" or spiritual instruction given by the Guru?

The word "upadesa" literally means restoring an object to its proper place. The mind of the disciple, having become differentiated from its true and primal state of Pure Being, which is the Self, and which is described in the scriptures as Sat-chit-ananda Being-Consciousness-Bliss), slips away therefrom and, assuming the form of thought, constantly pursues objects of sense-gratification. Therefore it is assailed by the vicissitudes of life and becomes weak and dispirited. "Upadesa" consists in the Guru restoring it to its primal state and preventing it from slipping away from the state of Pure Being, of absolute identity with the Self.

Bhagavan Sri Ramana Maharshi
*The Teachings of Bhagavan
In His Own Words* [p. 9]
*Sri Ramanasramam,
Tiruvannamalai, India, 1984*

Bhagavan Sri Ramana Maharshi

The Self Is Only Love

Question: Men of the world that we are, we have some kind of grief or another and do not know how to get over it. We pray to God and still are not satisfied. What can we do?

Bhagavan: Trust God.

Question: We surrender, but still there is no help.

Bhagavan: Yes. If you have surrendered, you must be able to abide by the will of God and not make a grievance of what may not please you. Things may turn out differently from the way they look apparently. Distress often leads men to faith in God.

Question: But we are worldly. There is the wife, there are the children, friends and relatives. We cannot ignore their existence and resign ourselves to divine will, without retaining some little of the personality in us.

Bhagavan: That means you have not surrendered as professed by you. You must only trust God.

Surrender to him and abide by his will whether he appears or vanishes. Await his pleasure. If you ask him to do as you please, it is not surrender but command to him. You cannot have him obey you and yet think that you have surrendered. He knows what is best and when and how to do it. Leave everything entirely to him. His is the burden, you have no longer any cares. All your cares are his. Such is surrender. This is bhakti.

Or, inquire to whom these questions arise. Dive deep in the Heart and remain as the Self. One of these two ways is open to the aspirant.

Question: Surrender is impossible.

Bhagavan: Yes. Complete surrender is impossible in the beginning. Partial surrender is certainly possible for all. In course of time that will lead to complete surrender. Well, if surrender is impossible, what can be done? There is no peace of mind. You are helpless to bring it about. It can be done only by surrender.

Question: Is surrender, by itself, sufficient to reach the Self?

Bhagavan: It is enough that one surrenders oneself. Surrender is to give oneself up to the original cause of one's being. Do not delude yourself by imagining such a source to be some God outside you. Your source is within yourself. Give yourself up to it. That means that you should seek the source and merge in it.

Question: But is God really the doer of all the actions I perform?

Bhagavan: The present difficulty is that man thinks he is the doer. But it is a mistake. It is the higher power which does everything and man is only a tool. If he accepts that position he is free from troubles, otherwise he courts them. Take, for instance, the sculpted figure at the base of a *gopuram* (temple tower), which is made to appear as if it is bearing the burden of the tower on its shoulder. Its posture and look are a picture of great strain which gives the impression that it is bearing the weight of the tower. But think. The tower is built on the earth and it rests on its foundations. The figure is a part of the tower, but it is made to look as if it is bearing the weight of the tower. Is it not funny? So also is the man who takes on himself the sense of doing.

Question: Swami, it is good to love God, is it not? Then why not follow the path of love?

Bhagavan: Who said you couldn't follow it? You can do so. But when you talk of love, there is duality, is there not – the person who loves and the entity called God who is loved? The individual is not separate from God. Hence, love means one has love towards one's own Self.

Question: That is why I am asking you whether God could be worshipped through the path of love.

Bhagavan: That is exactly what I have been saying. Love itself is the actual form of God. If by saying, "I do not love this, I do not love that," you reject all things, that which remains is *swarupa*, that is the real form of the Self. That is pure bliss. Call it pure bliss, God, *atma*, or what you will. That is devotion, that is realization and that is everything.

If you thus reject everything, what remains is the Self alone. That is real love. One who knows the secret of that love finds the world itself full of universal love.

The experience of not forgetting consciousness alone is the state of devotion (*bhakti*) which is the relationship of unfading real love, because the real knowledge of Self, which shines as the undivided supreme bliss itself, surges up as the nature of love.

Only if one knows the truth of love, which is the real nature of Self, will the strong entangled knot of life be untied. Only if one attains the height of love will liberation be attained. Such is the heart of all religions. The experience of Self is only love, which is seeing only love, hearing only love, feeling only love, tasting only love and smelling only love, which is bliss.

Be As You Are, Edited by David Godman [pgs. 85-88], 1985

Delight ... that which is beyond joy and that which gives meaning or purpose to life.

Delight ... is beyond sensation, or sensation is an attempt to translate the secret delight of pure existence itself, into the terms of physical consciousness.

It is the Bliss ... Ananda ...

of absolute conscious existence,

the supreme nature of omnipresent Being.

A. Ramana
Radical Realizations [p. 30]
AHAM Publications, Asheboro, North Carolina, USA, 1999

Ramana

Who's It Up To?

Opening statement made by Ramana to participants
attending the Self-Inquiry Seminar/Retreat at AHAM's India
Ashram on January 17, 2005

Ramana: This is a *very special* opportunity all of you
have these next two weeks, one that from the point of
view of a sincere spiritual seeker can be called "very
significant." It's an opportunity for your ultimate spiritual
awakening, or the realization and abidance in the true
Self. Are you into that?

Participants: Yes!

Ramana: Now consider this: just who is it up to for
this awakening to occur? How many "selves" are there
in truth – from the point of view of Truth, or with regard
to the One Reality?

Participants: One!

Ramana: Yes. And so, whose Self is it?

Participants: (In unison) Mine!

Ramana: You see, the simplicity of the matter is really
also the apparent problem, which is a strongly held
conviction and unanimously believed-in "personal" sense
of "I." This is not an accusation, but it's probably a
common fact with *all* of you.

Look for yourself ... and tell yourself the truth. Be
honest with yourself, right here and now! Does it seem
like there is an individual person, a personal sense of "I"
that you are identified with, think of as "me," a personal

"self" that's identified with this body and this mind that you call "yours," with a history or a "past" that seems to be living in time and space, that "was born" into time and space to "parents" also living in time and space, that each year is growing a year older and possibly a little wiser ... or maybe not? (Laughter)

Really look and see ... does this maybe define a scenario that you are identified with?

Now if it doesn't ... if you are *truly* aware that there's really only One Reality, only *one* Conscious Awareness, and that this Conscious Awareness is the One Self, and that it is manifesting *as* this world and *as all* these apparent persons, places and things appearing in various names and forms, then the question would be appropriate to ask, "Just what are you doing here?"

So again, I am not accusing anyone; I am just asking you to look for yourself, acknowledge what's going on with you, and tell the truth to yourself. You don't need to tell me the truth. It might be helpful though, to tell the truth openly, or to me. But, the main thing is to really tell *yourself* the truth, that there actually is with you this identification with the body-mind as being your "self," that you believe and feel as the sense of "me."

And, (consider this as yourself now speaking to yourself) in this identification that I have with the body-mind as being "me," I also see and acknowledge that I have no control over my identification with these constant thoughts, in the sense that random thoughts do rise up and take over my consciousness and apparently "require" me to identify with them, "require" me to believe and act on them, to be at the effect of them.

Now get this *if you are able to*: it is *not* the thoughts themselves that are the problem, it's your *identification* with them as being "me," or "mine," and your compulsive behavior of "going with them" or acting and reacting to them, in your identification with them. It is in fact your ego, identified with as being yourself, or as the true Self, which it is not.

These next two weeks you will be getting consciously in touch with your own Power of Awareness. Not to say you have not been in touch with it before, but you'll now be in touch with it in such a way to recognize it for what it *truly* is, and how to *purposely* utilize it. This means using this important power constructively, to henceforth be directed *by* It – efficiently and effectively – and bring about completion in all areas of your life. It's the ability to withdraw the mind back into your own Power of Awareness which is back into Itself, into the Source of consciousness Itself, to withdraw it back into the very Source of being and be free of all your suffering.

Now there may be some of you who question or challenge my saying this, who exclaim, "Hey, I'm not suffering, my life is pretty enjoyable." And I commend you if your life now happens to be that way. But in return I ask you, Can you depend on it being that way consistently, or *all the time?* Is there the potential or possibility that – due to the actual frailty of life as it is or is known to be – that this present "enjoyableness" of life in this moment could be disturbed? That tragedy could happen? That something could happen to your health?

It could happen to that which you know or think is giving you your present joy, maybe a relationship? That relationship might unexpectedly change, might be altered in a significant way, or end suddenly? Maybe that person changes his or her attitude or feelings toward you, leaves you, or maybe they die? Then, where are you? Would that alter your sense of well-being? Would that disturb you in consciousness, in your mind? Would you be able to remain beyond or prior to that, at peace, or without upset, and not be at the effect of that, *and genuinely so?*

If your true answer to that is, "No, I would be at the effect of that!" then you see that, yes, it may be fine that for now you can say your affairs, or state of mind and sense of well-being are quite pleasant, and therefore okay. But, recognize: the potential of losing that sense of well-being by some change, some event happening in your life, some major or even minor change occurring in the world around you, or to you, means that you are *really* still living at the effect of apparent life the world!

Again, this is *not* a judgement; I'm *not* accusing you. I'm pointing out simple facts, facts that are important that we all look at, and tell ourselves the truth about, "How do these things relate to 'me'?" Or, to the self you *think you are?* Is anyone with me? (Yes)

Now, everyone *truly* wants to be happy; and they want to be happy all the time, without the least taint of suffering, of sorrow, or loss, or upset. Am I correct in this?

Participants: Hm-hm!

Ramana: Everyone actually *does* want this. Well, that is the function and purpose of AHAM – the Association of Happiness. It is to share – with those that want this *uninterrupted* or *undisturbed* state or quality of happiness for themselves – the way and means to let this occur... which is by Awakening to the true nature of the Being that we are, the true Self that *you are... that we all are!*

You see, this quality of happiness will not and cannot come to you in and of and from the world. It's not to be found in the world – in any person, in any place or in any thing. It is just not there. If you think it is, you're only deluding yourself.

If you think and believe this – if up to now that's what you believe your happiness or your joy has been – I still say you're deluding yourself. Even when you now think that you're deriving happiness from some object, some person, some thing, some event, some situation occurring to you in the world... if you believe your happiness is actually coming to you from that thing *in itself* (whatever it may be), that *itself* is a delusion. It's a misconception. It's a false notion!

In such a moment – when an event happens that you feel has brought you happiness – if you stay conscious and are *very alert* as to what is *actually* transpiring at the time – you will recognize that in that moment your mind has briefly stopped. As a desired object is attained, or an undesired object is removed, your desire has suddenly stopped or subsided. When this desire momentarily stops, your mind stops. In that moment, your mind instantly inverts, or reverses itself and partakes of the quality of your own Being. That is, it then in the moment is not being hindered or disturbed by desire. The Self then "appears," or is temporarily "freed" to be expressed in the moment. In such moments, it is your own true nature being uncovered or revealed and you are partaking of it, your own natural happiness.

But then, very quickly – in most cases, almost immediately – another desire rises for something else, something more, or maybe something better, or something different in your life. And then you're off again on the quest for *that* desire. That next desire is itself now disturbing your natural peace, but you're not recognizing it, not seeing that you're actually disturbed by desire. This is because of the strategy or mechanism of the mind. It deceives you by concealing the Truth and the true Self from you and so you've learned to tolerate or "live with" the irritation of desire, which you have come to sublimate or convert into a more acceptable sense of stimulation. Does anyone know what I mean?

Seeking the fulfillment of desire is what "life in this world is about." It causes and sustains one's misidentification with the body-mind as being the Self, which we do not realize is also suffering, and the ongoing cause of suffering.

So what about one's desire for freedom from body-mind identification, or enlightenment? Paradoxically, the desire for enlightenment is itself in the end the one thing that is keeping us from it. Who is it that wants enlightenment? Wants realization? Wants liberation? Who is it that feels that you're not ... that you're not *already That* – enlightened, realized, liberated? Again, there's an "I." And this "I" feels like a unique individual awareness, identified with the body and the mind, limited to the body and it's environment, to the duration or lifespan of the body. But that is *not* the Self that you are. Instead, that's the self *you think you are* ... the self that you have been thinking you are throughout this entire lifetime, and many previous lifetimes before this apparent one.

Enlightenment is itself nothing more than the dissolving, if you will, of this individual sense of "I" back into the Source of Being Consciousness itself, merging in with the Source of Being, or Consciousness itself. Or it being dissolved and merged spontaneously on it's own, into the Source, or pure Consciousness itself.

What causes it? What causes this merging, or the awakening of oneself from or to this dream of mortality? What would you say?

Traditionally, it is said by the sages, and is acknowledged or confirmed by the ancient scriptures, that nothing you – you as a seeming individual being living in this dream of mortality, being identified with the waking-dream body (that is, this living physical body) and considering it as being the self – that nothing you yourself do, can or will awaken you from this mortal dream.

The truth is, that the world is an illusion; it's a dream, as is declared by the sages and acknowledged or confirmed by the ancient scriptures. But most people believe the world is a solid objective reality.

Now here is the scenario as described, or defined in detail: You as a character, as a player, as a "role" being lived in the dream and identified as such with both the dream and your role in it, are now believing that this world is solidly and objectively real, independent of you and your consciousness of it, and that you are yourself physically real as a separate individual living in this world. So, there is nothing that you as "a body-mind-ego" identified with it can do, to really end this configuration.

The truth is, it's all a superimposition. This whole scenario is superimposed on the One Presence, the One Reality, the Underlying Awareness that is the pure Self, the pure Being that we all are. There is only One, without a second. But, to this "self" you think you are, it looks and feels like there are many. And, this false perception, or misconception, is the one cause of all of our suffering. Can anyone relate to this?

Participants: (Nodding their heads, and quietly replying)

Ramana: So, what are we to do to be free from this suffering? Sri Bhagavan Ramana has shared with the world – or with those open and ready to hear it and receive it – a very unique way to actually awaken to this underlying Awareness or pure Intelligence. That Way is by tracing the primal Consciousness of "I" – the awareness itself that is ever alive and aware and awake in us (maybe not *always* "awake" in us, only in the waking and dream state) – by taking hold of it and intentionally tracing it, following it inward, or returning it back to it's primal, original nature. The other equally beneficial way or "method" is living in, or having the opportunity to be in close conscious company with someone who has *already* made and completed this quest, and who is now living in this pure Awareness of Being.

This next two weeks you have both of these Ways at your disposal. You will be trained in how to use the Conscious Process of Self-Inquiry properly and appropriately, and you will be in Conscious Company that will give you the opportunity to know what it's like to directly experience and *feel* this awareness as *your own actual true nature* – if you're not feeling it already or haven't knowingly felt it already. So you will be able to choose to remain in this awareness. You will be taken into the doorway, an opened doorway for you to move into this Awareness, experience this Awareness as your own awareness, and be able to choose to stay in this Awareness. It will be entirely up to you to make that commitment to yourself, to *stay* in this Awareness by intentionally utilizing the processes that you will learn, that we will be sharing with you.

All through this two weeks period, intently consider this simple fact: the self you *think* you are, the one you've been identified with, the one that seems to be "I" other than "you," whoever "you" happens to be (any "other") is *not* the Self you *really* are.

Keep reminding yourself, "The self that I *think* I am —
that seems to be a separate unique individual, different
from everyone else (meaning other than everyone and
anyone else and apart from the Source) — is *not* the Self I
really am." Keep awakening more deeply or clearly into
the pure Awareness itself, following it more deeply into
the very Sourcing Quality itself, the Sourcing Essence. You
can do this just by taking a firm hold of the sense of "I"
and tracing it inward, one-pointedly. And, by being here
in the charged atmosphere of this conscious company it
will be quite easy to do so. Nod your head if you are
recognizing it right now.

Participants: (All are nodding their heads)

Ramana: Being in this company, it's already easy to
"do." So, really "make hay while the sun shines." Stay
with the process. Keep your attention ever *in* the
Awareness that you *are*, NOT *on* what you're aware *of*. Even
if you're just aware of the "I," recognize that there's a more
pure awareness back behind or *prior* to this "I" that you're
aware *of*, which is the real Self, and you are not the
objective "I," you're the awareness that is aware of the
"I." Keep your attention ever on or in the prior awareness,
not what you're aware of. Watch the strategy of the mind
to want to identify with what you're aware of — what
you're conscious of — and thus get all caught up in
whatever it is that is happening in the moment in the
world, drawing your attention into it and making you tend
to be identified with whatever it is that you are conscious
of. Are you with me, do you get what I am talking about?

Participants: Yes.

Ramana: Diligently watch the strategy of your mind,
for yourself. Just get it; just keep watching it. And by
continuing to watch it, as the time unfolds in the training

itself, as Elizabeth gives you the processes, and you use the processes she gives you, you will find it to get easier and easier staying in this prior Awareness. For, it really is the Natural State.

It's always been the Natural State. It has never not been your natural state. There has never been a time in which you were not this Awareness. It's just that you've been covering it up with identification with the body and the mind as being "you." And having covered it up, you are now here to re-cognize it, to really *be* the Self that you are. Along with being identified with it, as "I-am-the-body" you are not recognizing that all of these so called "others" are only expressions of this One Consciousness, like waves in one ocean, and *you're* the ocean; you're *not* just a wave on the ocean. Stay with this process and you will have a profound experience!

Whether you recognize it or not, this is a "red letter" day for you. It could be the absolute end of your search. If it does not become the absolute end of your search, it can still be the relative end of your search because you will have come to the place where you recognize that you no longer need to search for any other way or method, because you will have already found the *most direct and immediate* Way to stay in this true Self-Awareness that you are.

And this is by the grace of Bhagavan Sri Ramana Maharshi, who has presented to the world this immediate and direct way into Self-Awakening and Self-Abidance. Are you with me? (Yes)

Good.

Namasté.

Abide as the Heart

Following is a guided meditation by Elizabeth:

Elizabeth: During a Heart Line call some months ago, after the guided meditation, we stayed silent the remainder of the program. There were no questions and no sharing; just a beautiful connection that can occur only in the Silence. It's interesting to be over the phone line and be connected so clearly with the Heart. There's nothing that seems to be in the way. No body here; just the Heart, just the Self. In the East it's called *Sat Sanga*, Conscious Company – company with Truth. It's like a tuning fork resonating a particular note, and when another tuning fork comes into proximity it can vibrate the same note. The "note" here in this *Sat Sanga* is the Heart.

Participant: I have trouble being still.

Elizabeth: Stilling the mind or stilling the body?

Participant: First of all, the body being totally still.

Elizabeth: Yes, in the beginning of meditation that's one of the things that the body has to get used to. Have you meditated long?

Participant: No.

Elizabeth: Ramana has spoken about his first encounter with meditation. He would sit for a few minutes and the next thing he knew he was up, opening up the refrigerator getting a soft drink. And all of a sudden he thought, "Wait a minute, I'm supposed to be meditating." And then he'd go sit back down again. It's something that you literally have to train the body to do. And after a time, with that kind of discipline, it succumbs.

That's one of the things we must face when we begin our spiritual practice, whatever that practice may be. Who's really been in charge up until now? ... My True Being? Or has this body-mind configuration been in charge? It's a rude awakening when we begin to see how much we're not in control of the body – that *it* has been the one in control.

When we get to the point of just accepting that the body-mind has been in control, we then choose the Self, the Heart, the True Me, the Pure Being that I AM, to be in control. That reversal takes discipline in the beginning, just like anything you do. If you're doing body-work or taking up a musical instrument, it takes discipline to get the body to do what you want it to do. It will initially challenge you. So you have to take charge. You choose.

Choice is a very big part of the practice. Many times we use our power of choice for things of the world: getting a new car, new house, new job, new relationship. In this practice, we use choice primarily, initially, to choose the Stillness, to choose the Silence, to choose freedom, and to choose to *remain* in and as that True Nature that we are.

Jesus said, "Seek first the Kingdom of God, and all else will be yours as well." It's the same thing, choosing the free space of Pure Being, the Heart. Then from Here, everything else will begin working for us. We begin the practice by making that choice.

So what are you choosing?

♥♥♥♥♥♥♥

Participant: Stillness.

Elizabeth: When you make the choice for Stillness, the power of choice that's within you – That which really Is You — will bring forth whatever is necessary in your life. You're utilizing that power of choice for your stillness, for your freedom. It's very powerful. So when you make that choice, make it with conviction. *"YES! I choose it. That's for me!"* Say it with fire in it. Take a stand ... *"Yes. It's time; time for me to remain in and be who I really am!"*

Can we all feel this? ...

♥♥♥♥♥♥

Participants: YES!

Elizabeth: Good. That's the point. That's the fire to get you started. And from then on, look out!

Participant: The steady, unshakable happiness that's your natural state, is that the freedom aspect?

Elizabeth: Yes, steady unshakable happiness. That's the term given, where nothing can shake you from being what you really are. Things may be happening in your life, but you are not shaken from your True Being, you are not reacting. You respond to life rather than react. That is our true nature; being in that place of true happiness, true freedom. It's already what's so, it's just a matter of locating it within you. Our attention has been going elsewhere. We've been thinking that happiness is in people, places, things, in the world. Happiness is our nature, just like the nature of water is wetness, it is our natural state.

Look to see how many times in the moment it looked like happiness, but always on the other side was pain.

The person went away, the vacation was over, the new thing got old. And here we are again, wanting something else. So when you find your true nature as steady, unshakable happiness, it doesn't matter what's there, what's coming or going, what's added to me or taken away. It really doesn't matter. I'm already complete, just as I AM. Feel this I AM ...

♥♥♥♥♥♥

Now we take the fullness of our happiness, the fullness of who we are, into our world, into our relationships, into our life; not expecting happiness *from* life, but bringing it *to* life. Then how can we be disappointed? How can we be hurt if we are not looking for happiness in our life, but we are bringing it to our life?

That's equanimity. You're able to be okay with what is so in your life. You're able to be very creative with what needs to be done. Some people believe that when you are in meditation, and abiding in the Stillness and the peace, that you're not really able to conduct your life responsibly, appropriately. But actually you are. You will stand up for yourself very matter-of-factly and creatively when you need to, without anger, without upset. Whatever needs to be done will be done. There's no disturbance; there is nothing in the way to keep you from going forward with what you need to do. So it's very practical.

One of the things that I've just love about Ramana who as you know originally taught me the Inquiry, is the way he's combined how to live in the world and still maintain your spiritual connection with the Heart. It's not your spiritual work over here, and your life over there, being two different things. They're in harmony together; they work side by side. That's very important in this western culture. We have our life to be responsible for, *and* we want to abide in our true nature. Why not? It can happen. It is happening with people that are following this practice.

We have people that come here who have never meditated before, and we have people who have been meditating for 20 and 30 years, and everything in between. So, it doesn't really matter where you are in your spiritual practice. What occurs during Sat Sanga is that you get the actual *experience* of who you really are, the Self. You get a good sense of what that is for you. In this way there is no gray area, doubt, or uncertainty about what to meditate on.

Self-Inquiry is exactly what it says – inquiring into one's Self. Most methods meditate on something objective: a candle flame, colors, sound, even a person. That's an object. And then eventually you will merge with the object you are meditating on. With Inquiry it's subject meditating on subject – Self meditating on Self. Aha … That's it! That's what I meditate on.

That's who I AM …

♥♥♥♥♥♥

Awakening can occur. It's very direct. It's very immediate. A shift occurs in consciousness, where you have the experience of being *behind* the body-mind, rather identified with it. Now you can function *from* the Self rather than from the body-mind.

♥♥♥♥♥♥

Sat Sanga is about hanging out with those who are already living the Heart, already living from the Self, so you will have the experience for yourself. Then your spiritual work is conducted from the Heart, *by* the Heart, from this point on, rather than being on your way *to* the Heart some time in the future.

Participant: Then are we wasting our time doing the meditation now?

Elizabeth: No. Any time you are sitting and being still, there is a benefit to you. So continue your meditation.

You can use a magnifying glass to direct the sun's rays onto a piece of paper. If it's just sitting out in the dry heat, it's not going to catch flame. But if you focus the sun's rays very directly in a fine point on the paper, it will catch flame. So this is what we offer here – a way that you can take the magnifying glass and find a tight focus, and really catch *fire* with the Self.

When you have an opportunity to be in Conscious Company *(Sat Sanga)* it's very beneficial in speeding up the process. It's a way to really focus that magnifying glass.

Sat Sanga happens here in conscious curriculum and in being in the company of our conscious community.

So it just depends on how quickly you want to move on in your spiritual work. Do you want it immediately, or some time in the future?

Participant: I still don't quite understand how being with someone else who is already enlightened helps me.

Elizabeth: Yes, it's kind of a mystery in the sense that in the West we're not as familiar with Conscious Company as they are in the East. Lets look at it this way – you can buy a lot of food at the grocery store, bring it home and put it up in your cupboard. You may know *about* food, you may know what ingredients need to go into a particular dish, but you just know *about* it. You haven't actually taken the food, put it in a pan and cooked it, served it on your plate and eaten it. You haven't had your own direct *experience*.

Some people can talk about being successful and have read a lot of books about it, but until they've actually experienced success, they can't really talk about success. So, when you're in the presence of someone already living it from the Heart, it's the difference between knowing *about* the Truth, and actually having the awakening for yourself. It's the same thing in your life. Does that make sense?

Participant: Yes, I understand that part. It really hit home what you talked about doubting whether you're doing it right or not. I'm always doubting, always questioning, "Is this what I'm supposed to be thinking? Am I coming from my Self, or the 'I' right now?"

Elizabeth: Another analogy came up when you talked about wondering if you are doing it right. If you wanted to learn to play a musical instrument to the best of your ability, wouldn't you go to a master – someone who was already accomplished in that particular instrument? It's the same thing. You find someone who is already living it. They are not just talking about it. Then while in their presence you can ask questions and they can guide you in the way to directly experience for your self ... You are always, already That."

The kind of direction you get from someone who is already living it is right on the mark. You're not wasting your time. It's not "the blind leading the blind." This person is already accomplished. And in our case, we have a community of people that you will be with who will be able to support you in that process. They will continue to remind you, "You are always, *already the Self, the Heart.* The only thing that is keeping you from being *That* is the thought that you're not already *That.* So by choosing to abide as the Heart, choosing freedom, choosing happiness, you can start bringing your attention back to the Truth of who you are."

Namasté.

About AHAM

Joe blushed and said, "I'm an independent distributor with a nationwide company that specializes in health and wealth. Mainly, I focus on new distributor procurement and educating them toward upper level advancement in our tri-level, unilateral, PV volume marketing plan."

"Oh," nodded Aunt Mary. "And, how's the wife and kids?"

Definitely a bust. Aunt Mary's eyes glazed over as she reached for more food. She probably didn't hear another word Joe said. Maybe Joe's answer was too expansive and complicated. Aunt Mary certainly didn't look interested in the conversation. In fact, the rest of the evening Aunt Mary kept her distance.

Later, Joe's old classmate Eric asked, "Joe, haven't seen you for awhile. What are you doing now?"

Joe thought, "This time my answer will focus on benefits. That will get prospects interested."

"Ah, yes. I'm an intellectual. I don't have
to do anything for a living."

Joe turned to Eric and said, "I'm independent now, in my own business of specializing in income diversification and incremental cash flow opportunities for potential entrepreneurs."

"Yeah, uh sure," Eric replied. "And, how about those Knicks? They're playing some pretty good ball lately."

Eric thought Joe's answer sounded like he might be a stealth insurance agent. Maybe talking sports would keep Joe from selling him a life insurance policy.

Joe drove home from the party. He thought, "Boy, what a dull party. No prospects there. None of those losers share my interest in MLM or getting ahead. I bet their idea of a good time is cable TV and popcorn. I wonder, where can I find some good prospects for my MLM business?"

One year later.

Joe's niece graduated this year. At the party Joe met his cousin Ben again. Joe asked, "Hey Ben, what are you doing nowadays? Still work for IBM?"

Ben answered, "I sell diet products that help people lose weight fast. Plus, I'm always looking for some additional help to spread the word. Seems more and more people today want to make some extra money on the side."

Joe replied, "Oh, really? How does the extra money part work?"

Ben explained about his MLM diet products and the MLM extra income opportunity. Joe commented, "You know Ben, I've been in MLM for years now. I never thought you'd be interested in MLM. I'm not interested personally because I already have an MLM opportunity, but I sure wish you success. By the way, why did you quit your secure job at IBM?"

Ben answered, "What security? I quit months ago. I'm full-time in MLM now. There's no security working for someone else. They can fire or lay off employees anytime they want. I feel a lot more secure now that I'm in charge of my life."

"What a change in attitude," Joe thought. "Last year Ben wanted to talk about the weather. This year he's an MLM maniac. I guess he could have been a good prospect after all."

Aunt Mary walked by with a plate of food. Joe said, "Aunt Mary, haven't seen you since last year. What are you doing nowadays?"

Aunt Mary replied, "I help people find good educational toys for their children and grandchildren. It's lots of fun and my MLM business is growing. I'm always looking for some partners who would like to make some extra money with me."

Joe gasped. "I never thought you'd get involved in MLM, Aunt Mary. What got you started?"

Aunt Mary said, "A friend of mine asked if I wanted to earn some extra money. Well, of course, I do. Doesn't everyone? And I love working with people, giving toy parties, sponsoring new distributors. It doesn't get any better than this. I only wish I knew about this a year ago."

"Low blow," thought Joe. "I had a chance to get her into MLM a year ago, but she didn't show any interest. What gives?"

Soon Joe's old classmate Eric drifted by with a portable TV in his hand. "Hey Eric, haven't seen you since last year. What's happening?" asked Joe.

"Knicks are up by 10 points. I won this hand-held color TV from my MLM company. Say Joe, did you know that there are two types of people in this world? Those who get a word-of-mouth advertising bonus check once a month . . . and those who don't. Which group would you like to be in?"

Joe stuttered, "The first group, of course. The ones that get those word-of-mouth bonus checks. I never really looked at things that way. However, I'm already in MLM and glad you're taking advantage of MLM too."

"Gee, what gives?" thought Joe. "I'm depressed. My best prospects were stolen by other people into their MLM companies. How cruel and unfair this world is." Joe left the party suffering from acute perverse prosecution complex.

The prospecting breakthrough

Joe stopped at his local hangout and ordered a beer (vitamin-fortified, with a secret blend of herbs and spices, and non-alcoholic, of course). Across the room Big Al just finished a two-on-one recruiting presentation. The prospect smiled, grabbed his new distributor kit, and ran out the front door excited about his new business opportunity. It must have been a pretty good presentation.

Big Al yelled across the room, "Hey Joe, how's it going? Run across any new prospects lately?"

Joe winced. "Low blow, Big Al. I just found out that three of my best prospects started their MLM careers recently — with competitors! They weren't the least bit interested when I talked with them. Life's unfair. Why do other people get all the good prospects?"

Big Al smiled. "Other people get all the good prospects because they have better skills. They don't practice stealth recruiting. Professional recruiters let people know what kind of business they are in and why their business would benefit the prospect. Joe, too many distributors never let their prospects know what they do for a living. Or, when they tell their prospects what they do for a living, they answer in generic, confusing, defensive, cryptic nonsense. Is that how you answer, Joe?"

"Generic, confusing, defensive, cryptic nonsense? Well yeah, that's sort of how I've been answering prospects who ask what I do for a living. Let me see. Last year at my nephew's party, all three prospects asked what I did for a living. I answered:

1. *"I work for the Wonderful Company, an international lifestyle focus corporation, in an executive distributor capacity.* Whoops, I guess there aren't many prospect benefits there.

2. *"I'm an independent distributor with a nationwide company that specializes in health and wealth. Mainly, I focus on new distributor procurement and educating them toward upper level advancement in our tri-level, unilateral, PV volume marketing plan.* Yeah, that's pretty confusing, cryptic nonsense.

3. *"I'm independent now, in my own business of specializing in income diversification and incremental cash flow opportunities for potential entrepreneurs.* Boy, that sounds like it's coming from a badly-dressed used car salesman."

Big Al said, "Joe, are you embarrassed what you do? Or, do you have trouble explaining what you do?"

"I love what I do, Big Al. I guess I just don't know how to explain it. I don't want to answer that I recruit new distributors, go to opportunity meetings, put on training sessions, retail product, listen to tapes, attend rallies, etc., etc., etc.. Sounds too complicated and hard, especially in a social situation."

"You're right, Joe. That's way too complicated. What do people want to know?

1. What you do, and
2. If what you do would be of interest to them.

"That's it. So why not answer their question with a strong benefits statement of what you do for a living?"

Joe scratched his head. "Sounds easy, but what would I say that would get people interested in what I do?"

"Let's see, Joe. You had three prospects sponsored by other people recently. **They must like what their sponsors said** — after all, they joined after hearing their sponsor's explanation. I bet they even use the same answer as their sponsor's when asked the same question. So, what did they answer when you asked them, 'What do you do for a living?'"

Joe said, "Well, they did have pretty strong benefit statements. Let's see . . . they said:

1. *"I sell diet products that help people lose weight fast. Plus, I'm always looking for some help. Seems more and more people want to make some extra money on the side.* Hmmm, there are two great attention-getting benefits there.

2. *"I help people find good educational toys for their children and grandchildren. It's lots of fun and my business is growing. I'm always looking for some partners who would like to make some extra money with me.* Yeah, Aunt Mary had two great attention-getting benefits, too.

3. *"Did you know that there are two types of people in this world? Those that get a word-of-mouth advertising bonus check once a month . . . and those that don't? Which group would you like to be in?* Wow! That benefit even got me excited.

"My three lost prospects gave great benefit answers when they were asked what they did for a living. They talked about how their product helped people and also checked to see if I was interested or looking for some part-time income. I'm starting to see a pattern here."

"That's right," continued Big Al. "You don't have to be offensive or pushy to let prospects know about your product's benefit or that you have a part-time income opportunity. Just mention what you do . . . and if the prospects are interested, they'll ask for more information. If they're not interested, they'll quickly change the subject to sports or the weather. Your interested prospects will have answers such as:

* "Hmmm. That's interesting. How does the part-time income thing work?"
* "What kind of diet products? Will it help us non-exercisers?"
* "Really, a part-time business that won't interfere with my work?"
* "Educational toys? I'm always looking for good gifts for my grandchildren."
* "Do you have to have any special background to do what you're doing?"

"All these replies are saying, 'I'm interested. Tell me more.' Isn't that a great feeling when people *come to you* saying 'I'm interested.' And, you don't have to be pushy."

"Right!" answered Joe. "Sure would make sponsoring distributors a lot more pleasant for me and for the prospects. So, all I got to do is change my answer into sort of a benefit statement, right?"

"You've got the picture, Joe. Your three former prospects had great benefit statements. Let's look at some answers to the question, *What do you do for a living?*"

* I show people how to get *bottled water* for only 3 cents a gallon.
* I show people how to lose weight without changing their eating habits.
* I show people how to have a high-vitamin, high-protein delicious breakfast drink for only 74 cents.

- I show people how to get rebates on their cleaning products.
- I help people get lower insurance premiums.
- I locate wholesale buying services so people won't have to pay retail.
- I show people how to get a rebate and referral check in their mailbox once a month.
- I'm working my own part-time business. I wanted something part-time that would help me get ahead financially.
- I always loved skin care, so now I give mini-facials to people who want to upgrade and try new skin care products.
- I'm still an environmentalist. Now, I change people's cleaning supplies to biodegradable cleaners. Plus, it saves people an extra $15 per month on what they're spending now at the store.
- I'm letting people know how they can get *wholesale* long distance rates, just like the big corporations. It saves folks about $20 a month on their regular telephone bill.
- I show people how to feel great, like they're 16 years old, but with better judgment.
- I put people on the fast-track to retirement. I save them money and help them retire 15 years early.
- I show people how to lose weight while they're eating cookies. Plus, they get paid to eat!
- You know, there are two types of people in the world, those who get paid to eat . . . and those who don't. Which group would you like to be in?
- Ever wonder if you might pay too much for something? I put people in contact with an 800 number where you get the guaranteed lowest quote on any item you purchase.

"See the difference Joe? All these answers give benefits. If the prospect has a need, interest, or desire, the prospect will ask you some questions. Those questions could lead to an appointment to talk in detail, or an invitation to an opportunity meeting. All we're doing is announcing the benefits. It is up to the prospects to sort themselves into those who are interested in knowing more, and those who aren't."

"I get it now," said Joe. "My generic answers really didn't say anything. There's no way a prospect could get excited about the confusing answers I gave. From now on, I'm answering with a strong, strong, benefits statement."

Big Al finished his drink (a caffeine-free, acid-free, biocatalyst nutritionally-enhanced coffee) and said:

"When you answer clearly with a benefit that may appeal to your prospect, you've produced a strong benefits statement. This makes the prospect *come to you* asking for more information. That's better than you pushing your information down the throat of an uninterested prospect. Plus, it's a more pleasant, low-key way to sponsor new prospects."

Joe got up to leave the local hangout. On his way out, he asked the bartender, "By the way, what do you do for a living?"

The bartender replied, "I provide a variety of alcoholic and non-alcoholic beverages to patrons in a social setting to help induce an acceptable climate for conversation exchanges to occur."

Clearly the bartender needed to talk with Big Al about his benefits statement.

Project

What do you personally do for a living?

Can you answer that question in one sentence?

Does your answer provide a benefit that will excite your potential prospects?

Here is what I do for a living:

_____

_____

_____

_____

The introvert's way to getting opportunity presentations

How would you like an unlimited number of people asking you "What do you do for a living?" Wouldn't it be nice? Your prospecting challenges would be over.

All you would have to do is recite your prepared *benefit-laden* answer. Imagine, instead of accosting strangers, running expensive ads, or irritating people with telephone cold-calls, you could do all your prospecting by answering the prospects' question: "What do you do for a living?"

So, how do we get an unlimited number of prospects to ask us, "What do you do for a living?"

It's easy. We simply first ask them, "What do you do for a living?"

No matter if you meet a person in an elevator, sit next to a person on an airplane, or just make an acquaintance at a social gathering, this simple questions works like magic. Your prospects' eyes dilate. They get excited. They get to talk about themselves. And, what's the number one, most interesting subject of your prospects? That's right. Themselves. They love to talk about themselves.

Not only will your prospects tell you about their work, but they'll give you blow-by-blow details of their last operation, the seamy details of their personal lives, their aspirations, their favorite sport teams, and their precise view on politics. All you have to do is listen as the prospects drone on and on about their boring, MLM-deficient lives.

Then, what happens after the prospects finally run out of breath? Out of courtesy, they usually ask you the question, "So, what do you do for a living?"

That's just the opportunity you've been waiting for. You give the prospects your benefit-laden description of your business opportunity or special product — and observe.

If the prospect says, "Hmmm, that's interesting. Tell me more," that's your signal to continue with your interested prospect.

If the prospect says, "Oh, that's nice. We sure have had a lot of bad weather lately," — well, that's your signal to go on and ask a different prospect, "What do you do for a living?"

How many qualified prospects do you want?

The amount of prospects who ask you what you do for a living is directly proportional to the number of prospects where you initiate the same question. So, if you want to have 10 prospects come to you with the question, "What do you do for a living?", all you have to do is ask 10 prospects that very same question. If you want 15 prospects, ask 15 prospects the same question.

Not only is asking this question effective prospecting, but it is also lots of fun. Since many prospects won't feel a need for your product or opportunity, you'll have the opportunity to learn about many new occupations, hear interesting real life stories, and have the chance to meet a variety of colorful people. And that's just the downside to using this technique.

The upside is you will find many ready, willing, and able prospects just looking for your opportunity or product benefit. These prospects will gladly set aside time for a presentation at their home or at a formal business opportunity meeting. These are the type of prospects that you won't have to beg to go to a meeting. They want what you offer.

This simple question really is a win-win opportunity. The prospects get an audience for their life stories and you get the opportunity to sort for qualified leaders. Life doesn't get much better than this.

How powerful offers can make your MLM business grow

Offer #1: Give me ten dollars.

Offer #2: Give me ten dollars or I will break both your knees, blow up your car, kidnap your spouse, scratch your CD's, and steal your dog!

You gasp, "Steal my dog? Oh, my! Here, take twenty dollars."

Some people are naturals when it comes to making powerful offers. Are you one of them? Or, do you make wimpy, wimpy offers that cure your prospects' insomnia?

In network marketing, we make offers every day. We make written offers if we advertise or use direct mail. We also make verbal offers to prospects. We ask them to buy our products, to come to an opportunity meeting, or to join our program.

On rare occasions, our prospects actually find the internal fortitude to refuse our well-meaning offers. They say "no" to our offer.

Let's take a look at our typical verbal offer to invite a prospect to an opportunity meeting.

Here's how our offer <u>sounds</u> to our prospect: "Come to our opportunity meeting and we'll take up two hours of your time."

Doesn't sound too exciting, does it? It's certainly not dripping with customer benefits either. We need to develop powerful offers that separate us from our competition. Our complacent competition isn't very tough, so if we do anything that is just 10% out of the ordinary, we're going to get great results.

If we don't sponsor our prospects into our MLM program at the end of our opportunity meeting, we should take a serious look at our offer. Maybe we are making a boring, weak, or inappropriate offer to our guests. Here is how most standard end-of-meeting offers are translated by our prospects:

♦ "Please join my MLM company." (Wow! My adrenaline is really cooking now.)
♦ "Please sponsor and get started today." (Yeah, so you can make money off my efforts.)
♦ "Give me $50.00 and you get to be a distributor." (Ooooooh, I can wait to reach for my credit card.)
♦ "You must get in today before everyone else gets into our business." (Gee, I really do want to be first in line at the slaughterhouse.)

No wonder our brother-in-law, our co-worker, and our hottest prospects say "no" to our offer to join. All four of these standard offers have had their benefits surgically removed by a lazy speaker. We need to give our prospects reasons and benefits. That is what makes powerful offers and rich MLM leaders.

Let's take a look at the standard opportunity meeting offer, "You give me money and I'll give you a kit." Definitely not too exciting, right? However, let's consider what would happen if, at the end of the opportunity meeting, the speaker would make the following offer:

"When you join this evening, you will receive our *Head-Start Success Package as follows:*

25

"**First**, you'll get a 200-page distributor training manual, a high-powered recruiting video to build your downline f-a-s-t, a product information cassette to help you get profitable retail sales, customer catalogs, applications, everything you need to start earning those big monthly bonus checks.

"**Second**, you'll receive *free* tuition to our $295.00 weekend training spectacular. There are limited seats, but you'll have a reserved seat in the second row. And the best part is . . . this upcoming training will be taught by the number one sales leader in the entire company. You'll learn how to qualify for the top bonuses in less than 30 days. This is a once-in-a-lifetime opportunity, and it's all *free* as part of your distributorship when you join this evening.

"**Third**, you will receive two *free* co-op shares in our weekly newspaper ads. You'll get to share in hot, fresh new distributor leads weekly. Don't worry, there's *no cost* because we're investing in your success.

"**Fourth**, you'll receive our team's *Confidential Insiders' Profit Manual*. It can't be bought at any price. We've invested tens of thousands of dollars in testing and improving these top sponsoring recruiting techniques, and you'll be one of the privileged few on the fast-track with this step-by-step manual.

"**Fifth**, you're going to get confirmed reservations for our next 12 leadership conference calls. You'll immediately be associated with the top earners in our weekly teleconferencing calls.

"**Sixth**, you'll get 10 certificates good for unlimited 3-way phone calls to sponsor your first 10 distributors. That's right, just call your hottest prospect, patch in your upline sponsor, and listen while your upline sponsoring leader helps enroll your prospect into your business. Now remember these are unlimited calls until you get your first 10 distributors. All you do is listen while you make money.

"**Seventh**, you'll be assigned a personal mentor, who will be your full-time consultant until you reach the top leadership position. You'll have constant access to the best help and advice our company can offer. And, all this is yours when you enroll tonight.

"And finally, **eighth**, you'll receive, absolutely free, our special introductory sponsoring cassette tape. Simply loan this informational cassette tape to friends and acquaintances. They'll have the opportunity to hear about how they too can join our fabulous business and get all our wonderful benefits."

Is there a difference between those two offers? Can you visualize prospects rushing to the speaker and saying, "Make me a part of this! This opportunity is for me!" Now when you bring your friend, relative or co-worker to an opportunity meeting, they will say, "Hey this is a fantastic opportunity," instead of saying, "Fifty bucks . . . I get a kit . . . yawn . . . no big deal."

So let's say you are a prospect in the real world and you had to choose between two opportunity meetings.

At the end of Opportunity Meeting A, the speaker says to you, "Here's the offer, you give me $50, and I'll give you a kit."

Next door is Opportunity Meeting B where the speaker offers you these eight incentives to sign-up as a distributor. You would say, "Hey I want to go to Opportunity Meeting B because that's where I'm going to get the best deal."

Now that's good marketing! *And the best thing is that it doesn't cost more to make the eight-benefit offer.* All of the incentives are *free.* We do all these benefits for our new distributors anyway. We run training meetings and help with three-way calling every week. We take these benefits for granted, but now we fully describe and package these benefits for our new prospects.

You see, we know all the benefits of our company. Unfortunately, we just assume our prospects know everything we know about our business. They don't. We have to romance our offers and educate our prospects.

Romancing the impossible

You can romance any offer and make it more effective. Prospects respond more to the romantic packaging than to the product or service. For example, MLM superstar Tom Paredes, author of *MLM War Stories*, used to be an Army recruiter. He could have described the Army opportunity as follows:

> It's like going back to primary school. You will get yelled at by mean instructors, you'll have no freedom, and all you can think about is how to escape from boot camp. We're talking institutional food here. Basic calories, no taste. Dress code? Heavy combat boots and dull, ill-fitting uniforms. If you live through your boot camp experience you can graduate to become a moving target for enemy sharpshooters. Oh yeah, did I mention the pay? You'll receive the absolute minimum allowed by law.

Not very enticing, is it? Of course, Tom Paredes repackaged his offer and added a little romance. This is how he presented the Army opportunity.

> Do you want fun, travel, and adventure? The Army will give you all that and more. In fact, they'll even pay you while you are having the time of your life. Think about it. You can travel to exotic places all over the world. And, you won't have to pay a single airline fare or hotel bill. The Army appreciates your participation so much that they even provide you with all your clothing needs with their unique designer fashions. Forget about those high clothing prices downtown. Never pay another health club membership fee again. You'll look forward

to supervised exercise instruction with a highly qualified personal trainer. You'll enjoy long nature walks and even your meals will be provided. Do you want even more excitement? The Army will place **live** ammunition in your hands as you celebrate your good fortune with fellow club members. And, as I said before, not only will the Army cover all your expenses, they'll even pay you money to insure that you are having the time of your life!

Hmmm. Which offer do you think recruited more prospects into the Army?

Final offer

Just a few minutes of planning can make your personal offers so much more powerful — your bonus income will skyrocket! All you have to do is make a resolution to set aside the planning time.

So, here's Big Al's final offer:

"If you don't start making powerful, benefit-dripping offers starting today . . . I'll shrink your bonus check, tell your friends not to join your business opportunity, take the chairs out of your meeting room, have your sponsor start calling you collect, and steal your dog!"

Project

What kind of offer do I make to my new prospects?

Can prospects understand the value of my offer, or is my offer using terms and concepts they are unfamiliar with?

Does my offer to new prospects give extra value if they start immediately?

What services do I normally perform for new distributors that I am not verbalizing in my offer?

My very best offer to a new prospect is:

_____

_____

_____

_____

_____

_____

Do I get excited with the above offer?

The secret word in great offers

Every sponsor says: "Join my company!", but they never say BECAUSE.

That's one difference between being selfish with no downline, and being a successful MLM leader with prospects lining up to join your group.

Instead of thinking of ourselves and our financial returns, let's think about our prospect and his potential reasons for joining.

The key to out-recruiting the competition is the magic word, BECAUSE. If we put that word at the end of our offer, it forces us to think of our prospects.

Instead of saying: "Join my downline!", why not say "Join my downline BECAUSE our co-op advertising campaign will guarantee you 11 fresh, new leads every week." See the difference?

Your MLM prospect will not join your downline for *your* reasons, but will join your MLM downline for his reasons. Help him out by giving him strong, specific reasons to join your downline. Here are some examples of reasons you could use, by placing these reasons after the word, BECAUSE:

+ We have weekly opportunity meetings 15 minutes from your house.

- ◆ I can give you full-time local support for in-home presentations.
- ◆ We concentrate on product knowledge and sales for a long-term, secure income.
- ◆ Our upline gives training sessions every Saturday.
- ◆ The last three people I sponsored, I helped each one earn over $800 a month permanent income.
- ◆ I will be your full-time employee to assist your growth towards the manager position.

Just remember the word, BECAUSE, and you'll be on your way to better downline recruiting.

The case study for better offers

Better offers not only work in personal contacts, but in advertising as well. Let's look at the power of better offers using a newspaper ad for our case study.

You decide to advertise for distributors for The Wonderful Vitamin Company. Your ad reads as follows:

ATTENTION ENTREPRENEURS
Become a distributor for
The Wonderful Vitamin Company.
Call now!

This newspaper advertisement cost you only $100. You received 10 responses to your ad. We know that not every response will join, but some will, most will not.

How much money did you invest to get a single response? Well you spent $100 for the ad, received 10 responses, so divide $100 by the 10 responses. Your answer should be that you invested $10 to get a single response.

Hmmm. That seems to be a bit much to get a phone call from a prospect. Why not try to get more responses from your ad? That will lower your cost per response and make your business more profitable.

You try the following ad which makes a better offer:

ATTENTION ENTREPRENEURS
Become a distributor for
The Wonderful Vitamin Company.
Call now and I will send you a *Free* copy
of the book, *The Wonders of Vitamin A!*

Because of a good relationship with the book publisher, you are able to get paperback copies of *The Wonders of Vitamin A* for only $3.

Your new ad with the better offer draws 50 responses. That's a lot more responses, but you did spend more because of your book purchases. Let's see what your total investment was for your new ad.

$100	advertising paid to the newspaper
$150	purchased 50 books at $3 each
$250	**total investment**

You spent $250 to attract 50 responses. That means your cost no longer is $10 per response, but only $5 per response ($250 divided by 50 responses = $5 cost per response). The improved offer of a free book motivated more readers to pick up the phone.

Now, that's better marketing. Cutting your cost per response in this case means that your advertising dollars can go twice as far. In other words, if you invest $1,000 in an advertising campaign, the first ad will bring you 100 responses ($1,000 divided by $10 cost per response). The second ad with the better offer will bring you 200 responses ($1,000 divided by $5 cost per response).

However, we are still utilizing old-fashioned marketing with weak offers. What if we talked to the book publisher and said: "Your book, *The Wonders Of Vitamin A,* really gets people excited about nutrition. I see you also sell books on Vitamin B, Vitamin C, and Vitamin E. Selling these books at their full retail price of $8.95 each could be very, very profitable for you.

34

"Here is what I suggest. Instead of paying cash for newspaper ads to promote your books, why not pay for your advertising with your books?"

"Hmmm," the publisher thinks. "If I paid for advertising with my books instead of cash, it would cost me less. I only pay $2 to get my vitamin books printed, so I'll be saving on my advertising costs. I'd much rather pay for $8.95 worth of advertising by giving someone a book that only costs me $2 to print. That's a lot better than paying hard-earned cash. It will like buying advertising at a discount."

You continue. "Here is what I recommend. Don't waste your money on newspaper advertising. Your best advertising is a satisfied reader who has already read one of your books. So, if you give me the book, *The Wonders Of Vitamin A* for only $1, I'll see that the book gets distributed to potential vitamin distributors for my company who answer my ads. Some of these responses will enjoy the book and order the rest of your fine books. Some will not. But, this will be a good way for you to advertise your books at a low, low cost. What do you think?"

The publisher says, "Why not give it a try? Sounds like a great idea. I'll reduce my cash outlay for advertising, plus I'll get some sample books into the hands of potential customers. Also, I'll still be receiving $1 per book to help cover my printing costs."

So, with this agreement in hand, you run the same ad:

ATTENTION ENTREPRENEURS
Become a distributor for
The Wonderful Vitamin Company.
Call now and I will send you a *Free* copy
of the book, *The Wonders of Vitamin A!*

Again, you receive 50 responses. What is your new cost per response? First, there is the $100 in advertising costs, plus, your new cost of only $50 for 50 books, *The Wonders of Vitamin A.* Total cost is $150 for your 50 responses. *Now, your new cost per response is only $3.*

While this isn't modern marketing, we are getting better. By lowering our costs to only $3 per response, we can now get 333 responses for our group to follow-up — for the same $1,000 advertising campaign. That's a lot better than our original $10 per response cost that would net us only 100 responses for the same $1,000 advertising campaign.

It gets better

You go to the local health club and ask them about their recent full-page newspaper ad that offered a free one-week membership. The health club proprietor says: "We offered a one-week free membership to get new people into our club. While they use our facilities during the week, our counselors educate them on the value of a one-year membership. Some of the guests join for one year, most don't. Trial memberships are a good way for us to get new, full-paying members.

"The full-page ad I ran in the newspaper was $1,000. From that ad, we usually get about 100 responses for a one-week trial membership. Let's see, if I pay $1,000 for advertising and get 100 responses, that means I'm paying about $10 to get a new, trial member."

You suggest the following . . .

"Mr. Health Club Proprietor, I have an idea. First, do you pay for your advertising in advance?"

He replies, "Sure do. The newspaper always wants its money up front."

You continue. "And, does the newspaper guarantee results for your ad?"

"No way. Sometimes I get a good response. Sometimes I get a lousy response. Either way, the newspaper gets the full amount up front."

You continue, "Well, I have a great idea. How would you like to pay exactly what you are paying now for a trial member —only $10 each. However, I can offer you at no risk, a guaranteed flat rate of only $10 per trial member that comes through your health club door."

The health club proprietor says, "That would be great. Could you arrange that?"

"No problem. And how would you like paying for your trial members AFTER they come to your health club? Wouldn't that be a lot better than paying the newspaper for advertising space in advance?"

"You bet! No risk, deferred payment of my advertising. Guaranteed results. Wonderful! So, how will it work?" Your health club proprietor is getting excited about your proposal.

You continue. "I'll run my regular ad in the newspaper advertising for vitamin distributors. In my ad I will offer a free, one-week trial membership for your health club. I'll pay for the ad in advance, take all the risk, and all you have to do is pay $10 for any trial memberships I send you after they arrive at your health club. Fair enough?"

The health club proprietor says, "I don't know how you can do this, but it sounds great. You've got a deal! I like the idea of guaranteed results, no risk, a flat $10 cost per trial member, and I even get to pay after they arrive. What a great deal!"

With the health club owner's agreement confirmed, the next week you run the following ad in the local newspaper:

ATTENTION ENTREPRENEURS
Become a distributor for
The Wonderful Vitamin Company.
Call now and I will give you
a *Free,* one-week membership
at your local health club.

Now the responses really start pouring in. People like a free one-week trial membership in a health club a lot better than a vitamin book. You get 100 responses to your new, improved offer.

Now, here is the big question. How much was your cost per response?

Let's see. First, you paid $100 for the newspaper advertisement. That was your entire investment.

Next, the health club proprietor gave you $10 for each of the 100 responses who accepted the free, one-week trial membership. So, you **RECEIVED** a check **FROM** the health club for $1,000.

Wait! You actually **MADE** money on your ad. You now have $900 profit ($1,000 from the health club less your $100 ad cost) **before** you even tried to sponsor any of the 100 responses. (Just think of your total profit picture when bonuses start coming in from the responses that you sponsored into your MLM program.)

You made $9 profit ($900 divided by 100 responses) per response. It no longer *costs* you to run recruiting ads for your distributors, it *pays* you instead.

So, could you give away these responses to your downline for a low cost? *For free?* Or, you could even pay your downline to give presentations to these ad responses. When you make a profit on your ad, the sky is the limit.

Now, if you made $900 profit on every recruiting ad you ran, before you even sponsored a single distributor, how often would you advertise? Monthly? Weekly? Daily?

Creating powerful offers makes a big difference. This is why some MLM distributors make fortunes while others go bald scratching their heads.

Plan your offers and your bonus checks will grow.

Better product offers attract distributor prospects too

We take too much for granted. After hearing dozens of product testimonials and tapes, and after reading exhilarating case studies of our product's miraculous results, we simply assume our prospect feels the same way we do about our product. Wrong.

Our prospects *want* to be sold on the benefits of our product. Nobody wants to buy boring, me-too products.

Imagine that we are selling Fat-Eaters, the herbal diet aid from the Wonderful Company. If we take our product and its benefits for granted, our sales presentation might sound something like this:

Distributor: Buy this bottle of pills. It costs only $29.95.

Prospect: I don't think so.

A prospect saying "no." Does this sound familiar? The prospect doesn't see any reasons or benefits of purchasing the mystery bottle of pills. We can turbocharge this mini-presentation by implementing these three techniques:

1. Tell the prospect exactly what your product does.
2. Add a little romance. Your prospect loves a story.
3. Make a powerful offer.

Let's give it a try. So, instead of saying, "Buy this bottle of pills. It costs only $29.95", say:

"You'll love these herbal fat-burning tablets. Just take two tablets first thing in the morning and you can feel the fat melting away while you enjoy your all-you-can-eat smorgasbord meals. Your body fat will vaporize as you channel-surf with your TV's remote control. Not only will your appetite be reduced, but you'll have so much energy that you'll feel like you are 16 years old all over again, but with better judgment. These fabulous herbal fat-burning tablets were a Russian secret, closely guarded by the KGB. However, Fat Thighs of America collected funds for a secret mission to steal this closely-guarded formula. After successfully smuggling this formula past the Iron Curtain and U.S. border guards, other obstacles had to be overcome. The Association of Overpriced Diet Clinics of America conspired to suppress release of this formula. They feared their overpriced gravy train of dieters would no longer need their services. But, the Wonderful Company defied the forces of evil, and accumulated enough raw materials to manufacture just three bottles of Fat-Eaters. Now, I'm making available to you, my closest friend, one of the three bottles in existence in the free world for only $29.95. And that includes the free book, *The Wonders of Vitamin A.*"

See the difference? Instead of announcing that we will trade a bottle of mystery tablets for $29.95, we:

1. Tell the prospect exactly what your product does.
2. Add a little romance. Your prospect loves a story.
3. Make a powerful offer.

Look at the improved offer from the prospect's point of view. People love to brag about their purchases and show off their knowledge. Comparing the following statements, which is more interesting when talking to friends?

A. I bought a bottle of pills for $29.95, or

B. Not only will I be losing weight while I inhale all-you-can-eat smorgasbords, but 14 secret agents lost their lives to bring this formula to the free world.

Will all our offers be this powerful and romanticized? No. We don't want to set off the *hype detection alarms* in our prospects with exaggerated claims.

However, we do want to make powerful offers. If our prospects love our product, they'll love our MLM business opportunity.

Here's your chance to put a little romance into your offer:

_____

_____

_____

_____

Sample offers to study

Let's take a look at some common offers. Many of these offers can be modified for your personal use. Allow your creative imagination to go to work.

Buy a new water filter for $39 down and $15 a month.

This offer takes away the price objection and minimizes the cost to the prospect. Prospects like to buy on terms. How many people pay for their home with cash? Most people make monthly payments on a mortgage. How many people purchase new cars for cash? Very few. Many people will lease or make car payments for four or five years.

Convenience and small monthly cash outlays make decisions easy to make. It is easier to make a $39 down payment decision than a $199 full price purchase decision.

Get super health and energy for only 50 cents a day.

Gee, that's less than a few cigarettes or a bottle of beer. This sounds like a real bargain.

The principle used here is called "reduction to the ridiculous." Your offer breaks the total cost of your product (health food or vitamin) or the total cost of your service (health club membership) into a small — almost ridiculous amount — to make the decision easier.

Let's say that your health club membership costs $180 a year. Now, that will demand a big decision from the prospect. To make it easy for your prospect to decide, you divide the $180 yearly membership by the 365 days in a year. That makes the daily cost only 50 cents, a much easier decision for your prospect.

Want to reduce the cost even more? Take the 50 cents a day cost and divide it by the 24 hours in a day. Total cost per hour? Only 2 cents. How could your prospect refuse super health and energy for only 2 cents per hour? Only two little copper pennies? Hey, your prospect probably doesn't even pick up the loose pennies he sees on the sidewalk while walking to work.

How can you use "reducing to the ridiculous" for your product or service?

Well, if you sell a $60-a-month diet plan, it only costs a measly $2 a day to be thin and beautiful.

If you sell a six-month supply of skin care for $100, it only costs your prospect just $16 a month! Or, your prospect can have young, healthy, great-looking skin for only 50 cents a day. Who wouldn't trade 50 cents a day to change their looks, turn back the aging process 15 years, or to rid themselves of acne?

If you sell a consumer buying service for $180 a year, it only costs your prospect $15 a month! Or, to put it another way, for only 50 cents a day, your prospect can be guaranteed the lowest wholesale prices on any purchase. Just two quarters buys peace of mind and guaranteed savings.

20% off all products in this catalog

This is a boring, unmotivated offer. Only 20% off? Have you ever walked down the aisles in a shopping center? What do you see on the windows? Signs pronouncing terrific sales. Some signs offer two-for-one offers or even three-for-one offers. You'll see signs of 50% off all inventory, 75% off everything in stock, or

80% off all summer wear. A 20% offer is a non-event — it won't get anyone's adrenaline pumping, no heart palpitations — only a yawn. You might as well keep the 20% in your pocket as long as you are going to bore your prospects anyway.

Come along to this evening's opportunity meeting and I'll buy dinner on the way there.

A great offer that especially appeals to overweight food connoisseurs. A good, filling meal helps the prospect relax (or sleep) during the opportunity meeting. At least this offer is better than the normal invitation which implies: Come along to this evening's opportunity meeting and I'll waste 2-3 hours of your time. Then, I'll high-pressure you into giving me money before I will give you a ride home.

Would you invest $100 in our program if we invested $200 in you?

How? You, your upline, and your company will invest $200 in training seminars, three-way calling, and person-to-person help sessions if your prospect is willing to invest $100 in a starter kit and product. This certainly is an improvement from the normal offer: Give me $100 for a kit and product and I'll be very happy.

You can lose 10 lbs. this month — without dieting!

This offer really promises benefits. If your product was an exercise bicycle, you could enhance and illustrate your major benefit by showing a picture of a satisfied user pedaling the stationary bicycle while eating a submarine sandwich. This offer goes directly to the prospect's heart with the promise of a 10 lbs. weight loss. Compare the above offer with a vague promise such as: Use our exercise bicycle to help you burn calories.

See the difference? *Specific* promises or benefits go straight through your prospect's mind clutter and gets his attention. Don't get lost in the fog of the 10,000 advertising images exposed to your prospect. Stand out from the crowd with a *specific* benefit.

"Bottled water" — only 4 cents a gallon!

Again we are "reducing to the ridiculous" to take away the prospect's fear of a large purchase such as a water filter. Plus, we grab our prospect's attention with the major benefit — "bottled" or high-quality, good-tasting water. The prospect doesn't want a water filter. The prospect wants clean, good-tasting water. This simple offer tripled one distributor's water filter sales in just three days.

Free 24-page booklet when you answer our ad

The word "free" does get attention and results for your offer. Using a premium such as a 24-page information booklet will increase your response.

How could we have made this offer better? By describing the benefits or romancing the information contained in the 24-page booklet. Our prospects really don't need an extra 24-page booklet at their house. Our prospects don't suffer from a 24-page booklet deficiency. However, they may want and desire to know what's in the booklet. So, let's re-word this offer.

- ◆ Free 24-page booklet describing how you can travel free to our exotic convention locations.
- ◆ Free 24-page booklet describing the many wonders of vitamin E.
- ◆ Free 24-page information listing of the top health spas in the United States.
- ◆ Free 24-page report on how you can cash in on the booming network marketing phenomena.
- ◆ Free 24-page step-by-step guide to retiring by age 50.
- ◆ Free 24-page instruction manual on how to use our power machine to lose weight.
- ◆ Free 24-page calorie guide when you order a 5-day diet program.
- ◆ Free 24-page tax strategy manual when you ask for our financial opportunity package.

- Free 24-page recipe book with your "Vegematic" appliance information package.
- Free 24-page mini-booklet showing the benefits of network marketing.

Get loads of prospects, customers, and new distributors by using specific benefit offers.

The above offer is for you. You'll need to create your very own money-making offer that will fill your savings account. Make sure you isolate a great benefit for your prospect. Then make your offer very specific. And finally, if your product is perceived to be expensive by your prospect, reduce the price to a ridiculously minute sum by showing the actual cost per day — or per hour.

So, here's your chance to write your great money-making offer:

_____

_____

_____

_____

So, what kind of offer should I make for my product or opportunity?

Good question. You had a chance in the previous chapter to write down some offers that you like. The good news is that you took the time to write down some offers. The bad news is that you wrote down offers that *you* liked.

A key to really great offers is to make the offer focused on what the *prospect* likes. That could be very different from your tastes, your goals, your desires.

For instance, let's say you are an MLM superstar. You have the big mansion, the chauffeur, the cars, and occasionally you charter an airplane to take the family to Aruba for a few days of sun. What would you want? Your own private Lear Jet so you wouldn't be at the scheduling mercy of your chartered plane.

Your desire for a Lear Jet could be quite different from what a prospect desires when he first enters multilevel marketing. Maybe your prospect desires a $500-a-month extra income to help pay for college expenses.

So, if you made an offer for prospects looking for your desires, such as a Lear Jet, you certainly would miss a lot of business opportunity-seekers looking for part-time income.

The point is, no matter how good we feel our offer is, the true test is how our market, our prospects would respond.

So, how do we find out what our prospects want? We ask them. This is our market research.

Who do we ask? Start by asking every prospect, who turned our offer down, the following questions:

- What didn't you like about my offer?
- What were you really looking for?

We should get some pretty good information from the prospects who refused our offer. However, don't stop there. Ask the prospects who joined our multilevel opportunity (or purchased our products) the following questions:

- Why did you join our multilevel opportunity?
- What was the main benefit that attracted you to our opportunity?

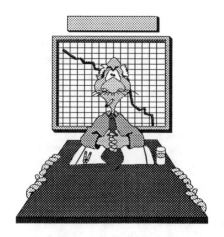

Weak or bad offers will make your bonus checks
plunge to unchartered depths.

Now we have some super information to construct our next offer. It doesn't take a rocket scientist to figure out that if one benefit is bringing in new distributors by the truckload, that benefit should be the focal point of our offer.

For example, let's imagine that Mary sells a diet product that gives you extra energy, and can also be shared as a business opportunity with prospects. Mary's offer to new prospects is:

I've lost 10 lbs. with my wonderful diet product. I have more energy. You too can get these benefits and make extra money sharing the opportunity with others.

Nice offer. Some prospects join. Most prospects don't. After interviewing some of her prospects, Mary discovered that their number one concern was having more energy. It seems their jobs were stressful. They were committed to many outside activities in

Great offers will accelerate your bonus checks
to new, higher levels of wealth.

addition to a busy family life and social life. Most of the prospects just wanted a solution to their fatigue.

Now, Mary repositions her offer to say:

> Get extra energy now! Stop being tired. You can feel great all day long. Plus, you can lose weight and earn extra money too.

Just by emphasizing the *energy* benefit more, Mary doubles her sign-up rate of new prospects. That's a 100% increase for the same amount of effort. So, is a little market research profitable?

You bet!

Smart fishermen know that if you go fishing for bass, use a bait that bass like to eat. Don't use your favorite food. It's the same principle in multilevel marketing. Make your offer emphasize what your prospects want.

Self-funding recruit-by-mail & advertising campaigns: The myth & the truth

Most recruiters want to know if they can break-even or make a healthy profit from their recruit-by-mail/advertising campaigns. Let's face it, we don't want to lose money, we want to make money. That's why most people enter MLM.

To understand "break-even", let's listen in on a telephone conversation with Big Al. It's from a not-so-famous, alleged expert, who is failing miserably as a recruit-by-mail fanatic.

To protect the guilty, we will call this mailing fanatic Homer. Homer wanted to recruit the entire United States on his new ground floor opportunity. Of course, this new ground floor opportunity was ten times better than the last ground floor opportunity which was better than the previous 20 ground floor opportunities this year. Hmmmm, it seems Homer picks ground floor opportunities that are only one-story buildings.

But, that's another story.

Anyway, Homer could make a bonus override of approximately $15 on every person who joined that month. He had just finished a 5,000 mailing where his letters, brochures, postage, printing and mailing expenditures totaled $3,000.

Homer: Let's see here. Looks like I will make $15 profit on every new recruit I get. So, to recoup my $3,000 investment, I'll need to sponsor 200 people from my mailing.

Big Al: You expect to get 200 new recruits from a 5,000 mailing? That's not a 4% response — that's a 4% sign-up ratio. Even mail order liars don't claim that kind of return.

Homer: The mail list broker said I should get at least a 10% return. He said that this was his very best, personal list, the one he never rents. He only sold it to me because he liked me. But heck, I read a chain letter yesterday and they even predict a 5% response on mailings. I know my new hot program is better that a chain letter.

Big Al: Have you tested your mailing offer yet? What kind of response did you get on your test to your personal list?

Homer: No, I haven't tested the mailer. I don't have a personal list because they are all mad at me as a result of the last program. Besides, I can write a letter that will pull in new recruits faster than I can open the envelopes.

Big Al: Have you tested the mailing list? Did you mail out a hundred or so first-class to see how clean the list was?

Homer: No time for that. This program is hot. I'm sure I shopped around for the best list possible. What are you, some kind of party pooper? What's with all this testing?

Big Al: Just thought it would be a good idea to check things out before spending $3,000.

From the initial conversation, things were looking bleak. Homer wanted 200 recruits to break-even on his mailing costs, and then expected an income for life while he sat by the pool. The price he was willing to pay? Five thousand letters through the mail. If life was that simple, everyone would be mailing 5,000 letters and quitting their jobs.

Three weeks later, the telephone conversation continued.

Homer: I lost everything. The list was bad. I have "return-to-sender" envelopes all over my living room. And nobody liked my offer. I only got four recruits. At $15 bonus each, that's only $60.

Big Al: That's not too bad of a start. Let's see where we can go from here.

Homer: What do you mean? I'm desperate for money to pay off my credit cards. And, I just heard about this great brand new ground floor opportunity that's really hot, a real money-maker. I need money to join this new deal before it's too late.

Big Al: Let's not be hasty. Breaking-even on an initial mailing is almost impossible, but at least you have a nucleus of four new distributors to earn a good return on your investment.

Homer: Even if all four distributors continue, I'll only earn $60 a month. At that rate, I won't break-even until four years from now!

Big Al: What about follow-up and training? Is it possible you might help them get their own downline started so they earn a larger bonus too?

Homer: Yeah, I see what you mean. If I can get one or two to build a group, my monthly check would go up to $400-500 a month. Maybe I should consider training and helping my new distributors. It's a novel idea, but it just might work!

Big Al: At $400-500 a month, you'd be making a profit in only seven months from this effort. Then, you'd be making pure profit thereafter. Not too bad, eh?

Homer: So, instead of looking elsewhere and joining yet another new ground floor opportunity, I should follow up my initial investment, right?

Big Al: Sure, but there's more. Did anybody write or call you for more information instead of sending their sign-up money?

Homer: I get it. I never contacted those people. I was too busy for curiosity seekers. You know, maybe I could recruit a couple of those hot inquiries too.

Big Al: And what about the people who looked at your program and didn't like it? What are they worth to a competitor?

Homer: You're right. If they hate my program but are interested in making money, maybe I could sell the lead or trade the lead with my local competitor. I'm sure he has similar leads I could use. Hey, I could break-even, even sooner now. You know, having four new distributors isn't that bad after all. But first, let me tell you about this new hot ground floor opportunity.

Big Al: Aaaaack!

"As a distributor, you'll learn about the 15 different incomes you can earn with **The Wonderful Company.** Besides retail profits, there's the downline group bonus, the 80% retailer's bonus, the General Major Sergeant-At-Arms bonus, enroller retail bonus, the daily GoGetEm bonuses, that's right, you can get a bonus check every day, the downline GoGetEm and the personal expense bonus.

"This marketing plan has been perfected over the years to provide **Wonderful Company** distributors a fast financial start in their own part-time business. And you don't have the normal expenses many small businesses have, such as large inventories, employees, rent and overhead. But there are more reasons why people become **Wonderful Company** distributors. Here's what other distributors say about the income opportunity . . . "

Women's Voice #6

"I listened to how a lady in Dubuque earns seven and eight thousand dollars a month selling just the *WonderFem* products. I'm happy just loaning out the video a couple times a week to make an extra $300 a month. This extra money makes my car payment. That's all I need from my **Wonderful Company** business."

Man's Voice #5

"I just wanted to be in business for myself and to control my own time. I never felt good asking my boss for time off or when I could schedule my two weeks' vacation. It was like being an indentured servant for 50 weeks a year. Now, I have both the income I need — and the free time I wanted."

Man's Voice #6

"I get a GoGetEm bonus check every day. This is in addition to the regular monthly bonus checks. One of my first level distributors got so excited about the GoGetEm bonus program that he earned $64 his first day, and $31 his second day. He hasn't even received his first regular monthly bonus check yet, but you know he's excited!

"I've been in multilevel marketing before and made money, but I like **The Wonderful Company** because not only can I get a good bonus check, but here, my downline can too. That's the difference. Everybody can earn good weekly and monthly bonus checks with this program."

Distributor #2

"There are two types of people in this world: Those who get paid to eat — and those who don't. From now on, every time you put food to your mouth, ask yourself, 'Am I getting paid to eat?' If not, maybe you should be a **Wonderful Company** distributor. My motto is: With **Wonderful Company,** you can eat your way to success!"

Man's Voice #3

"One of my friends has been a **Wonderful Company** distributor for several years. I joined, but never really got the vision. What got my interest? My sponsor made over $300,000 last year. Now that got my attention."

Women's Voice #6

"Everybody I talk to can either be a customer or distributor for **The Wonderful Company.** After all, who doesn't at least wash their clothes, clean their house, drink soft drinks, or use at least 60 or 70 different types of our products? And with retail markups up to 225%, I can make a great part-time income. I could almost make a living just by selling *WonderBrisk* to my friends with small children!

"In this business, there's always something new. Every time the company introduces a new product, it's like getting a pay raise."

Man's Voice #5

"To get ahead financially, you need to save a part of every paycheck and invest it wisely. But I was living from paycheck to paycheck and couldn't pay my bills. Now, the income from my **Wonderful Company** business pays my bills, plus funds my personal retirement plan. I'm no longer risking my retirement on just social security and the company pension plan."

Distributor #2

"The secret key is to help your distributors become successful. I've only sponsored a handful of people but now have thousands and thousands of distributors in my downline. You're only as successful as the people you help. You don't have to be a super salesperson or recruiter with this business."

Man's Voice #6

"Too many people depend on the lottery — or dream of being adopted by rich, dying millionaires as their plan for financial success. Five years — ten years from now — they'll still be in the same shape they are today. Their dream home becomes a dream condominium, and then becomes a dream apartment.

"It's sad, because all they had to do to change their future was to get involved with **The Wonderful Company.** I think this is the greatest plan in the world. My question to others is: 'What plan are you following? If your plan isn't working for you now, why not change to a proven plan that works?'"

Announcer's Voice

"There are many reasons to become a **Wonderful Company** distributor. Some people want better health. Others want a secondary income in case they lose their primary income through layoff or branch closings. Still others want an exciting full-time career and to be in control of their time.

"What do you want? Or better yet — what do you have to lose?

"Don't wait forever. Now is the time to really get ahead. Join now with the thousands of successful **Wonderful Company** distributors to build your financial future and dreams."

(Music Fade)

END

Triple your A.S.K. (Automatic Sponsoring Kit) results

"Nyah, ah, ah!" Sleaze Shallowman's evil laugh announced another brainstorm. Besides lacking the morals of a disbarred lawyer congressman turned credit card fraud artist, Sleaze was "1+1=3" dumb. If there was a way to foul up a good system with stupid shortcuts, Sleaze would be your man.

"Why wait for success? And, why work hard passing out Automatic Sponsoring Kits one-by-one? I'll just get my 365 Automatic Sponsoring Kits distributed in one day!" Sleaze was excited. Let the rest of the network marketers toil away meeting prospects one-by-one. Let them work hard. Sleaze had a brilliant plan.

First, Sleaze located the zip code of the wealthiest community in town. "Might as well go to where the money is," thought Sleaze. Then, he chartered a small plane and pilot.

Early the next morning, Sleaze loaded his 365 Automatic Sponsoring Kits into the small plane. After a quick take-off, Sleaze showed the pilot which neighborhood to fly over. When the plane was in position, Sleaze opened the cargo door and dumped the 365 Automatic Sponsoring Kits onto the neighborhood below.

"Crash, ka-pow, thunk!"

The saturated bombing got the neighborhood's attention. Some of the Automatic Sponsoring Kits crashed through living room windows, some dented a few cars, but mostly they littered front lawns, gardens and driveways. "Hee, hee, hee," snickered Sleaze. "It will be hard for those prospects to ignore my Automatic Sponsoring Kits!"

True, the neighborhood didn't ignore Sleaze's saturation bombing. His answering machine was filled with angry callers by the time he returned home. Maybe this automated mass marketing campaign wasn't going to be so great after all.

The bottom line? Sleaze handled 180 complaints and did not receive a single interested inquiry to know more about his business. Ouch! Another brilliant shortcut to success proves to be a dead end.

What went wrong? Lots. However, the two main principles Sleaze forgot were:

◆ When giving a prospect an Automatic Sponsoring Kit, a lot depends on *who you are.*
◆ When giving a prospect an Automatic Sponsoring Kit, a lot depends on *what you say.*

These two principles can triple your sponsoring results. Let's see how to put them to work for us.

Who you are

Imagine you are walking down the street and you see a drunk standing in the gutter. He has a bottle of cheap wine in one hand and is using his other hand to hold onto a parking meter, to keep his balance. This drunk shouts unprintable expletives to the pedestrians passing by. A small dog walks by and the drunk kicks the dog across the street. When you pass this drunk, he gives you an Automatic Sponsoring Kit.

What is your reaction?

Will you listen to the audio cassette tape? Will you eagerly track down the drunk the next day to ask for some marketing advice and additional information? After evaluating the drunk's living habits, what would you think of the business opportunity's ability to change people's lives?

If you're normal, you might pass up this particular business opportunity. You might be thinking what it would be like to invite your drunk sponsor over to your house for a business opportunity meeting with your friends.

However, there may be nothing wrong with the business opportunity described in the drunk's Automatic Sponsoring Kit. It might be a wonderful opportunity, but you won't pursue the opportunity because of *who gave it to you.*

What if the late George Washington, the first president of the United States, was standing on the same street? As you passed George, he gave you an Automatic Sponsoring Kit.

Now, what would your reaction be?

You might think, "Hey, George is a pretty classy guy, a real leader. I think I'll check-out this audio cassette tape and literature and see what George is into nowadays. This could be pretty interesting."

See the difference? Same opportunity, same Automatic Sponsoring Kit. The only difference is *who* gave you the Automatic Sponsoring Kit. In the first example you received your information from a drunk, while in the second example you received your information from someone you respected.

The better the person (sponsor), the better the results.

If we want better results when we give a prospect an Automatic Sponsoring Kit, all we have to do is become a better person. No matter where we are today, we can always improve. How? Here are just a few ideas:

- Attend every company training meeting
- Get your sponsor as your mentor
- Take self-improvement courses
- Read self-improvement books
- Listen to self-improvement tapes
- Find out more about your product line.

First, become a better person. Then, you will get better results. It doesn't work the other way. You can't get better results and then decide to become a better person.

It's like the old riddle about the rich man who had a fabulous library. Some people would say, "Sure, I could be rich too if I had a fabulous library like that rich man." However, the truth was that the man became rich because he gradually accumulated and learned from his library.

It's the same for us. We get better results after we become a better person.

What you say

That's the second principle to getting better results when giving a prospect an Automatic Sponsoring Kit. We can pre-sell, give a sense of urgency, and motivate our prospect to listen to our audio cassette tape and to read the included literature.

When Sleaze Shallowman saturated the neighborhood with Automatic Sponsoring Kits, he never said a word to prepare his prospects. If we simply stand outside of a grocery store and stuff our kits into shopping bags as customers leave, they'll have little incentive or interest in reviewing our audio tape and materials. There's no relationship, no communication, no reason for the prospect to care about us or our opportunity.

However, imagine we gave a prospect an Automatic Sponsoring Kit and said, "The audio cassette tape has a great idea on earning some extra part-time money."

This simple sentence primes the prospect and gives the prospect a reason to take time to listen to the audio cassette tape.

Could we do better? Sure.

Maybe we notice that a lot of our prospects procrastinate and never get around to listening to the audio cassette tape. When giving the prospect the audio cassette tape we could say, "Let me know what you think of the tape. I'll come by and pick it up tomorrow night, okay?"

We just put an artificial time limit on our prospect's review time. Our prospect feels he should quickly listen to the audio cassette tape before tomorrow night. Or, our prospect might say something like this as a response: "Tomorrow night? Ooops. I won't have time because I'm having university final examinations tomorrow. Is it okay if we get together for lunch on Monday and talk about it then?"

Either answer is fine. We just wanted our prospect to commit to a review time. If we left the review time up to the prospect, he would delay his review for weeks — or even months.

Want a few ideas on what other multilevel distributors say when passing out their Automatic Sponsoring Kits? Here are a few mini-presentations to prime your imagination:

"You won't believe how this lady made over $1,500 part-time in less than six weeks. You'll really enjoy what she says on this tape."

"Most people dread April 15th, the tax deadline. Want to hear how a couple of accountants beat the system?"

"Guess what? There's a system where anybody can lose 10 lbs. quickly without dieting or exercise! You can listen to the details on the way home in your car."

"Want to invest sweat equity instead of risking money in your own business? You'll like the ideas on this tape."

"This tape shows a powerful way to make some extra money. After listening to the tape, could you do me a favor? If the extra money idea doesn't interest you, could you pass the tape along to another person?"

See the difference? Just a few words, a sentence or two, can really pre-sell your prospect to immediately listen to your audio cassette tape.

This is why giving a prospect an Automatic Sponsoring Kit *in person* can be so effective. Can the Automatic Sponsoring Kit be used as a response package for an advertising inquiry or a direct mail inquiry?

Sure. It certainly is better than mailing some brochures and hoping for the best. However, the Automatic Sponsoring Kit is **not** as effective when used as a cold, initial mailing package. Renting a 365-name mailing list and adding some postage usually meets with disappointing results.

The big problem is that you have no relationship with these out-of-state strangers who suddenly find an audio cassette and some business opportunity literature in their mail box. Put yourself in these strangers' shoes. Do you wake up in the morning and say to your spouse, "Gee. I sure hope we get some boring literature and an audio cassette tape in our mailbox today. I don't plan to go to work, there's nothing good on TV, and we do need something in our mailbox to hold those bills down so the wind won't blow them away."

Most people have lives. Unfortunately, their lives don't revolve around us. You don't know the people on this rented mailing list. They don't know you. They don't respect you. They don't care about you. They think you are some junk mail nut committing arborcide and filling up landfills with your solicitations. They say to themselves, "Hey, if your opportunity was so good, why couldn't you get anybody you know to listen to you? Or, why couldn't you get anybody locally? Do the locals feel you have a lousy reputation, or what? Is that why you have to resort to soliciting strangers in another state?"

Having no relationship with these strangers means you can expect to receive no respect and no results.

Person-to-person is the best way to distribute your Automatic Sponsoring Kits. Your prospects can attach the business opportunity with a real person — you. Plus, you get an opportunity to pre-sell the prospect.

Using the Automatic Sponsoring Kit as your response package to advertising or direct mail replies makes sense too. These prospects are expecting information from you.

And finally, if you want to triple your sponsoring success rate using Automatic Sponsoring Kits, remember the two key principles:

- When giving a prospect an Automatic Sponsoring Kit, a lot depends on *who you are.*
- When giving a prospect an Automatic Sponsoring Kit, a lot depends on *what you say.*

More A.S.K. (Automatic Sponsoring Kit) strategies

What are the first two things that new distributors want to know when they join your MLM opportunity?

- ◆ They want to know **where** they can find new prospects who they can talk to about their new business.
- ◆ They want to know **how** to talk to these new prospects.

Some distributors are afraid to talk with their warm market of family and friends because they feel that they have inadequate presentation skills. Or, maybe the new distributors just want to avoid personal rejection and want to market the opportunity to total strangers.

All these challenges can be solved by using the Automatic Sponsoring Kit. New distributors no longer have to give full presentations or try to convince their warm market to join their new business opportunity. All they have to do is to give their warm market an Automatic Sponsoring Kit and let their prospects decide if the opportunity is for them.

No personal rejection. No hard sell closing. The business of sponsoring becomes a simple task of allowing prospects to review information and qualifying themselves.

Your new distributors can see themselves prospecting successfully. Just the availability of an Automatic Sponsoring Kit might have been the key reason your new distributors joined. Your new distributor probably thought:

> "Why join an ordinary business opportunity where I will have to quickly master presentation skills, make cold calls, and get constant rejection? This business opportunity has an Automatic Sponsoring Kit that will make my business profitable and easy. This is the business opportunity for me."

The Automatic Sponsoring Kit will make your personal recruiting easier.

You need appointments

What is the key activity in building your business once you have distributed your Automatic Sponsoring Kits? Appointments. Without business opportunity presentation appointments, you're out of business.

Think of it this way. How much money would your dentist make if he didn't have any appointments? How much money would the local hairdresser make without appointments? Without appointments, most professionals are *unemployed.*

Appointments are the yardstick to measuring effective activity in a multilevel marketing business. When you have a downline distributor complaining about low activity, small bonus checks, and how hard it is to work the business, simply ask that distributor, "How many business presentation appointments did you set last week?"

Usually, they answer, "None." They were busy watching cable TV, going to a football game, arranging their inventory, reading a book, or thinking about all the reasons they can't be successful in their own business.

This simple question, "How many business presentation appointments did you set last week?" takes the wind out of their sails. It puts the real activity necessary to do this multilevel marketing business into perspective. No appointments, no business.

I had one complaining distributor come up to me and say, "This business really stinks. I only signed up one new distributor in the last eight weeks!"

So, I asked, "How many business presentation appointments did you set-up last week?"

The complaining distributor answered, "Just the one."

End of conversation.

What's the easiest way to get appointments for your business opportunity presentation? Simply loan out plenty of Automatic Sponsoring Kits.

Do you want more great recruiting ideas?

Call (281) 280-9800

Or write to:

KAAS Publishing
P.O. Box 890084
Houston, TX 77289

http://www.fortunenow.com

We'll send you a **_free_** copy of our training journal with free sources and tips.

Here Are <u>Four</u> More *Big Al Recruiting Books* You'll Want In Your Library:

#1 *Big Al Tells All, The Recruiting System (Sponsoring Magic).* This is the original *Big Al* classic that details the entire *Big Al* Recruiting System. You'll learn about:

- Locating and qualifying new prospects
- Closing before you start your presentation
- The two magic questions
- Making fear of loss work for you
- The dairy farm syndrome
- The 25-minute presentation that works
- Strawberries as a selling tool
- Ridding your organization of the ten deadly myths
- And much, much more

This is the <u>perfect</u> <u>book</u> to **fast-start** your new distributor. If you were to read only one *Big Al* book, this should be your first choice.

#2 *How To Create A Recruiting Explosion.* This book contains more advanced recruiting techniques such as:

- Locating the fishing hole for the best prospects
- Too good to be true
- The checklist close - the easy way to decide
- Trade show challenges and rewards
- Finding the best people
- Ad techniques that work independently
- Handling questions
- Street smarts
- Solving office problems
- And the all-time blockbuster recruiting technique, *The Stair Step Solution!* This is the way to build 20 to 30 new distributors *F-A-S-T!*

#3 *Turbo MLM.* Accelerate your group-building with this third book in the *Big Al* Recruiting Series. Turbocharge your recruiting methods by using:

- The million dollar close
- Mail order recruiting
- Handling money handicaps
- Sorting for true leaders
- Tale of two winners
- Dangers of over training
- Why prospects don't join
- And, the all-time super income builder: ***The Presentation Ratings Game.***

#4 *How To Build MLM Leaders For Fun & Profit.* Build massive downline organizations by building independent motivated leaders. Your group is only as strong as its leaders. Special sections on:

- Cloning superhuman leaders
- The $93,000 Recruiting System
- Piggy-back your opportunity
- Ninja mail
- The file drawer method
- Hype from the top
- The 2% myth
- How to get all the prospects you want
- Streamlining your business for extra profit
- Man Kills Family Pet principle
- And much, much more

Volume Discounts

All **Big Al** Recruiting Books are $12.95 each. For the professional leader who wishes to take advantage of *Big Al's* surprisingly generous quantity discounts, the following schedule applies for ***any combination*** of his five books:

10-24	$6.95 ea.
25-49	$6.00 ea.
50-99	$5.00 ea.
100-499	$4.25 ea.
500 or more	$3.95 ea.

(Note: There is a $3.00 shipping charge per <u>order</u>.)

Order from:

KAAS Publishing
P.O. Box 890084
Houston, TX 77289

http://www.fortunenow.com

**American Express, Visa, MasterCard, Discover orders
phone (281) 280-9800 or fax (281) 486-0549**

Recruit New Distributors Fast!

Over 240,000,000 Americans presently do not participate in MLM. Now you can sponsor this huge, untapped market with our newest recruiting tool, *Are You Walking Past A Fortune?*.

This 24-page mini-book sells your prospect on the benefits of MLM. All you do to start an effective recruiting campaign is:

1. Pass out this 24-page mini-book.
2. Wait a day or two for the prospect to read the book.
3. Pick up the book and sponsor the prospect.

The mini-book does the selling for you. Many of your prospects will be eager for you to guide them into an extra income opportunity in MLM. A few of the prospects will give the book back to you and admit they aren't interested. You spend your time with the eager prospects.

So make your recruiting career easy. Stop spending money on expensive ads, exotic mailings, or cash-depleting direct mailings. Let *Are You Walking Past A Fortune?* sort your prospects so you can spend your time helping those who want your help.

Are You Walking Past A Fortune?
30 copies for only $12

Order from:
KAAS Publishing
P.O. Box 890084
Houston, TX 77289

http://www.fortunenow.com

American Express, Visa, MasterCard, Discover
orders phone (281) 280-9800 or fax (281) 486-0549

Feel a bit shy when approaching strangers? Would you like to turn acquaintances into hot, eager prospects? How can you approach potential prospects about your business without looking like a greedy salesman searching for a quick commission?

How To Get Rich Without Winning The Lottery, by Keith Schreiter is easy to read, easy to implement, and shows how anyone, a carpenter, a rocket scientist, a housewife, or even a lawyer (gasp!) can follow the simple principles to accumulate wealth. And the best part is that this book will show your prospects how to add network marketing to their wealth plan if they wish.

This is a gift that will build a long-term relationship. So leave a copy of this book with that cab driver who gave you good service, to that hotel employee who helped you set up your opportunity meeting, to the waitress with the million-dollar smile, and to your best friend who would like to be rich, but doesn't knew how.

Once you read this book, your life will never be the same. You'll be on the direct road to financial independence even without the help of network marketing. And because you already do network marketing, you'll be way ahead on this million-dollar road to riches. The book is so good, you won't want to give away your personal copy.

Give the books away?

Yes. These books were meant to given away as gifts that will instantly bond you with your prospect.

And the price? A little more than $1 each in quantities. About the cost of an audiocassette tape, but so much more impressive.

The proof is in the results. First, you'll personally love the book as it will quickly direct you to the most direct road to wealth. Second, you'll love the instant relationships this book creates with your prospects. Now you have something really important to talk about. And third, the book pre-sells network marketing so that your prospect is ready to take advantage of your business opportunity.

Single book	$4.00 each
2-99 books	$2.50 each
100-499 books	$1.38 each
500 –999 books	$1.29 each
1000+ books	$1.23 each

Order from:

KAAS Publishing
P.O. Box 890084
Houston, TX 77289

http://www.fortunenow.com

American Express, Visa, MasterCard, Discover
orders phone (281) 280-9800 or fax (281) 486-0549

Big Al's MLM Sponsoring Secrets is Big Al's complete audiocassette tape library with the very best recruiting techniques for you and your downline. The information is awesome and easy to use.

Eight brand new audiocassettes with Big Al's best recruiting secrets. Plus, you get <u>four additional</u> audiocassettes with his basic training workshop, *Big Al Live in London* — free. The entire set of 12 audiocassette training tapes can be ordered by sending $69.00 to:

KAAS Publishing
P.O. Box 890084
Houston, TX 77290

http://www.fortunenow.com

Visa, MasterCard, Discover and American Express orders
Phone (281) 280-9800 or
Fax: (281) 486-0549